The Persecuted Church
In the Late Twentieth Century

Also by Ann Ball:

Holy Names of Jesus

A Litany of Mary

Modern Saints: Their Lives and Faces

Modern Saints: Their Lives and Faces (Vol. 2)

The Persecuted Church
In the Late Twentieth Century
Ann Ball

with chapters by:

Rev. Paul Marx, O.S.B.

Stephen Dunham

magnificat press
Avon, N.J.

The Persecuted Church
Copyright 1990 Ann Ball
All Rights Reserved
Printed in the USA
ISBN 0-940543-10-9
Library of Congress catalog number: 89-092410

Magnificat Press
315 Main St.
Avon, N.J. 07717

"Inside Malaysia's Persecuted Church" by Rev. Paul Marx, O.S.B., first appeared in Human Life International's special report no. 66, copyright 1990 Human Life International, 7845-E Airpark Rd., Gaithersburg, MD 20879.

"Threats to the Church in the United States" by Stephen Dunham, copyright 1990 Magnificat Press.

Maps: Mary Lane

Dedication

For my children,
Joanna and Sam,
who inherited freedom,
and for Philip and Louis
and all who fought for America's freedoms,
and for Bill and Mike,
who know the law
and practice it justly,
and for my country,
"Sweet Land of Liberty"

Thanks to . . .

Betsy Altenburger, St. Agnes High School, Houston, TX.
Heather Horn, Houston, TX.
Rev. Richard Flores, Sacred Heart Church, Seymore, TX.
Rev. Athanasius Pekar, O.S.B.M., St. Josaphat Seminary, Washington, D C.
Professor Nestor Rodriguez, University of Houston, TX.
Bishop Enrique San Pedro, Diocese of Galveston-Houston, TX.
Rev. James Gaunt, University of St. Thomas, Houston, TX.
Glen Burleson, Houston, TX.
Rev. Jim Hurley, S.D.B., editor, *Salesian Bulletin*, New Rochelle, NY.
Rev. Timothy Burkauskas, O.S.P., National Shrine of Our Lady of Czestochowa, Doylestown, PA.
Ginte Damusis, Director, Lithuanian Information Center, Brooklyn, NY.
Rev. Don Willis, The Methodist Church, Houston, TX.
Rev. and Mrs. Alain Racourt, Miami, FL.
Miss Mary Decker, Houston, TX.
Mr. and Mrs. Mike Hickey, Friendswood, TX.
Kindra Bryan, Houston, TX.
Mike Murphy, Houston, TX.
Rev. Jim de Loach, Second Baptist Church, Houston, TX.
Hugo Sanches, Watauga, TX. . . . and all the others whose help and encouragement have made this book possible.

Contents

Introduction	1
Albania	7
Bolivia	11
Bulgaria	15
Burma	19
Burundi	21
Cambodia	25
Chad	27
Chile	29
China	35
The Congo	45
Cuba	47
Czechoslovakia	53
El Salvador	59
Estonia	65
Ethiopia	67
German Democratic Republic	69
Guatemala	71
Guyana	73
Haiti	75
Hungary	81
Iran	87
Laos	89

Latvia	93
Lithuania	95
Malaysia: "Inside Malaysia's Persecuted Church" by Rev. Paul Marx, O.S.B.	101
Malta	107
Mexico	109
Mongolia	113
Mozambique	115
Nepal	123
Nicaragua	127
North Korea	131
Poland	133
Romania	143
South Africa	147
Sudan	149
Turkey	151
U.S.S.R.	153
Vietnam	167
Yugoslavia	171
"Threats to the Church in the United States" by Stephen Dunham	173
Selected Bibliography	183
Organizations supporting the persecuted church	185

"...More Christians have been killed [martyred], I believe, during the last 50 years than perhaps in any other period in the history of the Christian Church. Many Christians are not aware of how strong the anti-God movement is in the world."

—Billy Graham,
"Christ Will Return"
Decision magazine, June 1990

Introduction

The Constitution of the United States was, and is, a daring document. Immediately after its drafting, it became a symbol of hope and freedom for oppressed peoples all over the world. The first order of business for the fledgling country that promised freedom and justice was to create a Bill of Rights for the citizens; it was submitted to and ratified by the states in 1789. This Bill of Rights, the first ten amendments to the Constitution, was written to protect the citizens from tyranny, and to ensure some areas of personal freedom where the brilliant founding fathers felt that the government ought not to trespass at all. The first of these golden guarantees of freedom reads as follows:

> Congress shall make no law respecting an establishment of religion, or prohibiting the free exercise thereof; or abridging the freedom of speech, or of the press; or the right of the people peaceably to assemble, and to petition the government for a redress of grievances.

We tend to take for granted our freedom to worship, but all over the world, in numerous countries, clergy, members of religious orders, and lay Christians are thrown into prison, beaten, and tortured. Their crime? Their belief in God. Some religious sects have practices that may cause legitimate concern for the better welfare of the citizens as a whole; however, all Christian and Jewish adherents have as a basic part of their theology an emphasis on peace. Yet today Christians and Jews alike are often harassed and persecuted.

Jesus said, "Blessed are you, when men shall revile you, and persecute you, and shall say all manner of evil against you falsely, for my sake" (Matt. 5:11). He also said, "Love the Lord your God with all your heart, soul and mind. This is the first and greatest commandment. The second most important is similar: Love your neighbor as much as you love yourself" (Matt. 22:37-39).

Let us show our love for our persecuted brothers and sisters by our prayers, our petitions, and by publicizing their plight. We *are* our brother's keeper.

Jesus told His apostles, "Beware of men: they will hand you over to the Sanhedrin and scourge you in their synagogues. You will be dragged before governors and kings for My sake, to bear witness before them and the pagans.... You will be hated by all men on account of My name; but the man who stands firm to the end will be saved" (Matt. 10:17-18, 22).

The Apostle Paul said, "I now rejoice in my sufferings for you, and fill up in my flesh what is lacking in the afflictions of Christ, for the sake of His body, which is the church" (Col. 1:23). Bishop Enrique San Pedro, auxiliary bishop of the Diocese of Galveston-Houston, when discussing persecution, pointed out that the problem is more widespread today than people think. He said that first you must define persecution. There has been overt persecution found in the Soviet countries and China and Vietnam, but there is also covert persecution, common in Latin America. In some places where the government is strongly of one religion, such as Muslim or Hindu, Christianity is persecuted by simply being disallowed. Additionally, the persistent prejudice against the Catholic church in the news media and other places in the United States can be considered a type of religious persecution. "There is more than one way to kill a man," San Pedro said. "You may shoot or stab him with a knife, or poison him, or simply slowly take away the oxygen needed for respiration."

Father Jim Hurley, S.D.B., editor of the *Salesian Bulletin*, wrote, "As in China and Eastern Europe, so in Cuba and Nicaragua, we find that when a Marxist regime cannot drive religion from the hearts of the people, they will try to isolate the church from the people. Typical ploys include government screening of seminary candidates, government appointment of pastors in 'national security zones,' expulsion of foreign-born clergy except those outspoken in support of the Marxist government, and finally establishment of a 'national hierarchy' without obligations or ties to the Roman Pontiff."

"The early Christians were filled with reverence for their brothers who had suffered persecution for Christ's sake. The Mass was celebrated over their tombs in order to underline the spiritual union between living Christians and the martyrs. For the past seventy years, the Church has been suffering a persecution wider in scope, more refined in its methods and crueller than any other persecution of the past," wrote Father Werenfried van Straaten, O. Praem.

Cardinal Joseph Tomko, head of the Congregation for the Evangelization of Peoples, in a radio interview in Italy in August 1987, pointed out that Catholic missionaries have been killed at the rate of about one per month since 1980, most of them because of their faith. He attributed the killings to a renewed climate of violence in many parts of the world. Tomko said, "In the last several years, there has been a fresh outbreak of both bloodless, systematic persecution in some Third World countries, as well as a certain aggressiveness and violence that leads to killings." He pointed out that church statistics show about seventy missionary killings between 1980 and 1985.

Dr. David Barrett, an Anglican priest who is a noted religious statistician and editor of the *World Christian Encyclopedia*, reported that an average of 330,000 Christians a year are martyred for their faith around the world. His research has led him to conclude that one of every 200 Christian workers is being killed on the mission field. He pointed out that approximately 95% of the situations of martyrdom go unreported in the media, and therefore unrecorded. Dr. Barrett defined a martyr as "a Christian who loses his life for Christ in a situation of witness as a result of human hostility." He defined a Christian as "anybody who is a believer in Christ."

A few of the reports in this book deal with persecution of religious groups that are non-Christian or on the fringes of Christianity, such as Jehovah's Witnesses and Mormons; those few have been included because they illustrate governmental attitudes toward religion in general, and merit our concern.

Each year, the Senate Committee on Foreign Relations and the House Committee on Foreign Affairs jointly publish a report on Human Rights Practices throughout the world. This report is a statutory requirement, and is published to assist members of Congress in considering legislation in the area of foreign assistance. Although the report documents all areas of human rights, it does consider religious freedom as a separate category in each country where information is available. Information from this report has been used as a primary source in research for this book.

Organizations such as Amnesty International, Keston College, Pro Fratribus, Free the Fathers, The Persecuted Church Commission, The Catholic League for Religious and Civil Rights, The Lithuanian Information Center, Helsinki Watch, and a number of others take an active role in disseminating information about our persecuted brethren in other countries. By publicizing the plight of those who are persecuted for their faith, they hope that changes can be made in the various countries.

This book is not intended to be a comprehensive index of persecution of Christianity in the world today. Rather, it is intended to give an overview of the problem and demonstrate its magnitude. The problem of persecution is here, and it is serious. Although the situation throughout the world is continually changing, I have done my best to bring the facts up to date as of early 1990, including the rapidly changing situation in Eastern Europe. According to the organization Aid to the Church in Need, "The 40-year oppression in Eastern Europe is coming to an end." Nevertheless, while the future looks much brighter for religious freedom in those countries, the situation there is uncertain. Also, persecution continues in many other communist countries. The massacre in Tiananmen Square in Beijing, China, shows that an apparent relaxation of government control does not always end with liberty in full flower.

In early 1990, Congressman Christopher Smith of New Jersey, as a conressional delegate to the United Nations General Assembly, asked the U.N. Human Rights Commission to investigate brutality against religious believers in many nations, citing China and Nepal as candidates for investigation by the U.N. "If left to their own devices, countries potentially will go off and continue their persecution," he told an Associated Press reporter.

I hope that the reader will, through the examples given here, be inspired to pray for peace and freedom in the world, and to contribute as best he may to the effort to relieve the sufferings of our persecuted brethren in Christ. Although Christ promised that His followers would be persecuted for His name's sake, He also promised salvation for those who persevered in their Christian belief. Additionally, He commanded His followers, "Love your enemy." As we share our love, concern and prayers with those who are persecuted, let us also pray for their persecutors. Jesus taught, "There is a saying, 'Love your friends and hate your enemies.' But I say: 'Love your enemies! Pray for those who persecute you!' In that way you will be acting as true sons of your Father in heaven" (Matt. 6:43-45).

ESTONIA
LATVIA
LITHUANIA
GERMAN DEMOCRATIC REPUBLIC
POLAND
CZECHOSLOVAKIA
HUNGARY
ROMANIA
YUGOSLAVIA
BULGARIA
ALBANIA

Albania

The constitution of Albania, as well as government policy, prohibits all religious activity. In 1967, Albania proclaimed itself the world's first officially atheistic country and began an active campaign to completely eradicate all vestiges of religion from Albanian life. At that time, approximately thirty percent of the population were Christians. Churches were closed, religious leaders were persecuted, imprisoned or executed, and laws were passed to prohibit any religious publishing or personal manifestations of belief. Baptism is a criminal offense. Parents may not give Christian or Muslim names to their children. A few historic churches have been restored, along with their religious art, as museums, but the majority of religious buildings have been converted to other functions.

The regime has never let up on its suppression of religion, nor its harsh treatment of believers. To insulate the population from foreign religious influence, Albanians are forbidden to travel abroad except in an official capacity. In spite of twenty years of religious persecution, however, there are reports that some Albanians quietly continue to practice their faith in their own homes, especially in rural areas. A 1988 report by the Puebla Institute, "Religion in a Fortress State," noted that Albania was still attempting to eradicate religion.

The official Albanian government press denies that believers have been persecuted, and maintains that religion is only opposed by argument, not reprisals. In 1983, the Vatican publicly condemned Albania for its religious persecution and reported that a number of priests, members of religious orders, and seminarians had died in prison, as well as two priests having been executed for conducting baptismal rites.

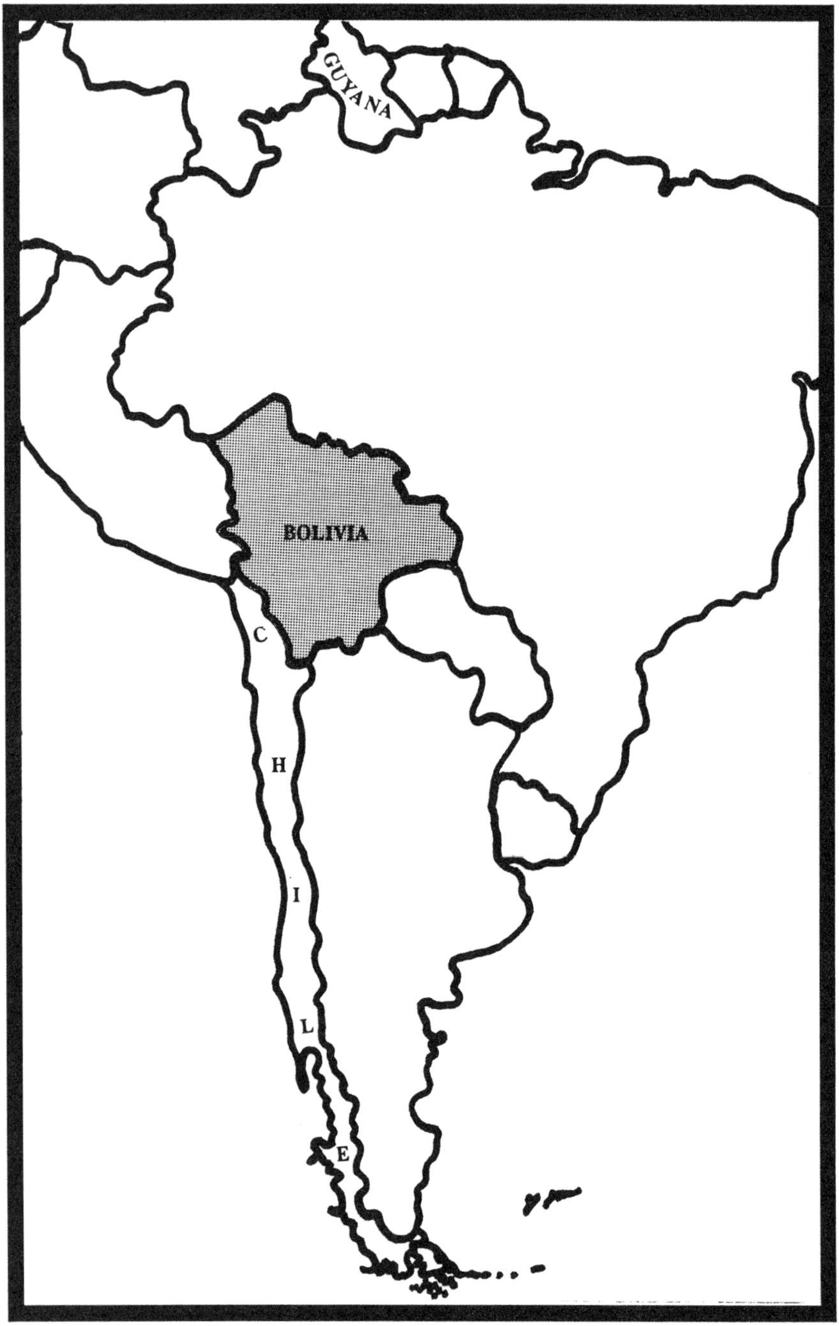
GUYANA
BOLIVIA
C
H
I
L
E

Bolivia

Although churches in general are allowed to practice freely in Bolivia, the law does require that they be licensed, giving the government the power to expel those sects they find troublesome.

In February of 1986, an official protest was received from the Bishop of Oruro. Six unidentified men, one in a policeman's uniform, had broken into the residence of the Oblate fathers and with no judicial order searched the house on the pretext of searching for a Colombian. The Bishop of La Paz also protested that local government officials had been harassing Radio San Miguel and church officials in the Department of Pando. In June, state security personnel raided the library of a Jesuit high school and beat and detained some of the students for a short time. In August, a Catholic priest, some seminary students, and two Methodist ministers and a leading Methodist theologian were detained on suspicion of subversive activities.

The Catholic Bishops' Conference and the Methodist church have both been vocal in criticism of what they see as incidents of official hostility.

In November, five government agents broke into a Franciscan convent to look for marijuana plants. The agents apologized when no marijuana was found, but the Archbishop of Sucre registered a formal protest.

* * *

The world is almost coherent without God.
And God remains silent,
He does not defend himself when insulted,
Nor does He loose His thunderbolts when they
 deny Him.

Everything is silent,
But it is a hostile silence.
And when we pray,
Our prayer seems without dialogue;
It's a howling of the wind
In an abandoned house.

But God hears our anxiety
Even though He seems far . . .
O Lord of silence,
We offer you our loneliness,
Our absolute loneliness,
For even now
You are not absent.
We don't have anything more intimate,
And more ours.
We offer you our finiteness,
The roots of our being;
We offer you the anxiety of being human.

* * *

The above lines were written by Father Luis Espinal, a Jesuit priest who died in Bolivia in 1980. Father Espinal offered God his finiteness in his poem, and his life in reality.

Father Espinal was born in 1932 in a suburb of Barcelona, Spain. He was ordained in 1962, and served in Spain until 1969, when he was sent to La Paz, Bolivia. Little by little, Father Espinal began to realize the problems of Bolivia, and the causes of the poverty and misery of many people. He identified with them and began a campaign to denounce social injustice and defend the poor. He was involved with a number of causes, and in particular he denounced the leaders of the mafia and the narcotics trade in the country.

On the night of March 21, 1980, Father Espinal disappeared. His fellow priests and the father provincial became worried and began to search. The following day, his body was found abandoned near a small village. The body showed signs of terrible torture, with numerous bullet holes.

Father Espinal's remains were transferred to the chapel of the San Calixto College in La Paz, where a large number of people came to view the remains, mourning and praying. The assassins have not been discovered, and the crime was not investigated.

Many conversions among the youth and the poor, all over Bolivia, are attributed to the sacrificial death of this priest. He is held up as an example of one who kept his Christian social principles until the end. He gave his life for his brothers—the poor and those in need. The wide distribution of his writings and his poetry are seen by many as a clear sign that God did not want his life forgotten. Hidden in the heart of the South American continent, the fire of Luis Espinal's imitation of Christ, and of his evangelism, still burns brightly in the work of those who have so generously continued to work for the reign of God in Bolivia.

ESTONIA
LATVIA
LITHUANIA
GERMAN DEMOCRATIC REPUBLIC
POLAND
CZECHOSLOVAKIA
HUNGARY
ROMANIA
YUGOSLAVIA
BULGARIA

Bulgaria

The recent political upheaval in Bulgaria appears to be bringing improvement to what has been a bad situation for the Church. Theoretically, the constitution of Bulgaria provides for freedom of worship. In fact, the authorities espoused atheism, discouraged and regulated religion, and considered openly expressed religious convictions a deterrent to any type of advancement. Church-state relations were regulated by a committee organized under the Ministry of Foreign Affairs. The committee reviewed all clerical appointments and often took direct action with regard to these. Most types of religious instruction were forbidden in practice. At the Communist Party Congress in 1986, new policy directives against religion were adopted.

The Bulgarian Orthodox church is the largest and most accepted religion in the country, receiving some government funds and limited other rights, and in turn has echoed government propaganda on a number of themes, such as peace and disarmament.

It was illegal to import Bibles, and a 1986 government report mentioned that customs officials had on a number of occasions intercepted Bibles and religious pamphlets. A Bulgarian-language Bible was last printed in 1982, with only 2,000 copies being distributed. In 1983 and 1984, two priests were allowed to study in Rome. When they returned to Bulgaria, however, the religious materials and Bibles they brought back with them were confiscated. Most denominations have complained about the lack of printed religious materials.

Older worshipers were generally not interfered with by the authorities when attending services, but police periodically harassed younger attendees and attempted to discourage them from attending. In 1984, on Easter eve, members of the militia harassed young persons who were trying to enter a service at a local church in Sofia. Also in 1984, some young people were required to obtain passes from the Communist Youth Group to attend church services.

Roman Catholics constitute a small group, with both the Latin and Uniate Rites being represented. A number of small Protestant churches also function. Priests and ministers have been careful to avoid political and social rights themes in their sermons. No open proselytizing or foreign missionary activity was permitted. It was against the law to provide formal religious education to children, although some young people do attend services with their parents.

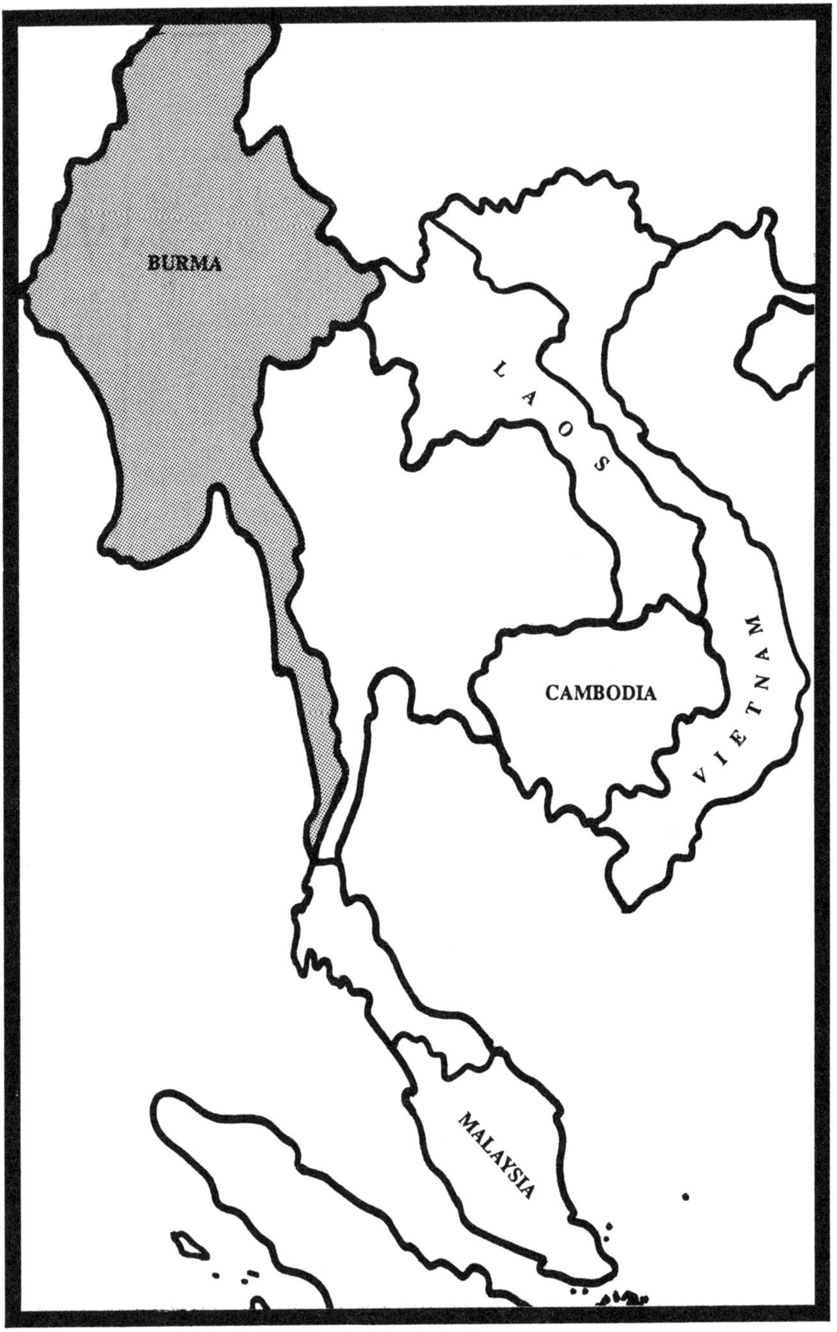
BURMA
LAOS
CAMBODIA
VIETNAM
MALAYSIA

Burma

All religious groups are generally allowed to practice freely in the Socialist Republic of the Union of Burma. However, foreign religious representatives are usually allowed only tourist visas and are not allowed to preach or proselytize, although a few foreign missionaries who are long-time residents of the country are allowed to remain with their congregations.

Also, the law requires religious organizations to register with the government, and religious publications are controlled and censored by the government. On occasion, a nationalization law has been used to allow the government to take control of the property belonging to religious organizations.

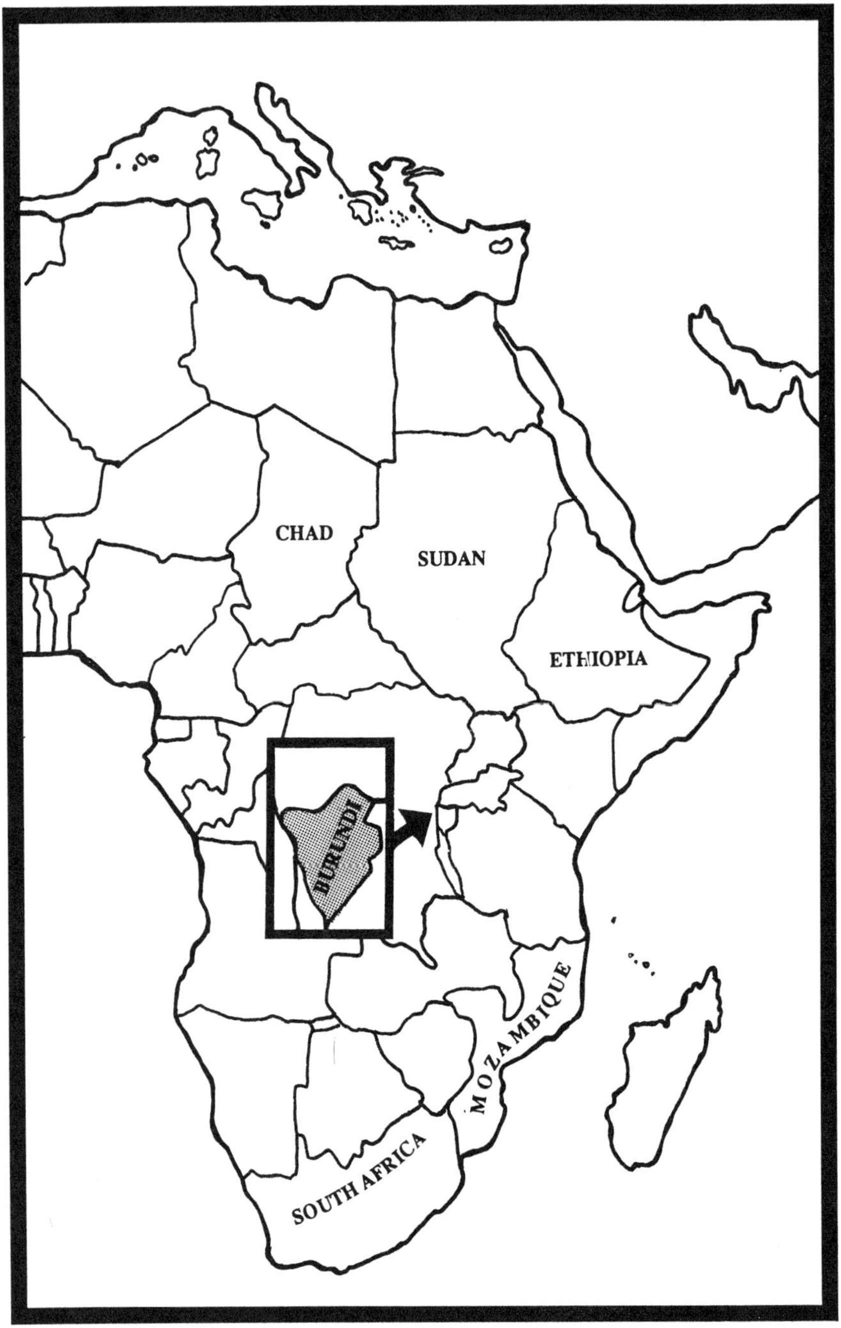
CHAD
SUDAN
ETHIOPIA
BURUNDI
MOZAMBIQUE
SOUTH AFRICA

Burundi

In Burundi, religious freedom has had strictly defined limits until recently. All religious associations needed government approval to operate. Religious groups were expected not to engage in political activities critical of the government. The government required advance notice of all religious services, and strict time limits were set on these. In addition, religious services could only be held in recognized places of worship.

The Seventh Day Adventists' refusal to work on their sabbath, Saturday, led to the closing of their churches and schools and the loss of their legal status in 1985, and in the first half of 1986, forty-seven Adventists were arrested for failing to perform governmentally required community service on Saturday mornings. The forty-seven were released, but later two others were arrested for the same reason.

About ten other Christian religious leaders and laymen were arrested in 1986 for refusing to respect government restrictions. They were released shortly after their arrest, all within a few weeks. But two Catholic priests were arrested for criticizing the government, and are still in jail. Over two hundred missionaries have been expelled since 1985, and many more have left voluntarily, leaving fewer than two hundred foreign missionaries in the country. Church schools and most seminaries were placed under government control in 1986, and many clerics were relieved of their teaching positions.

Church-sponsored literacy classes in rural areas were suspended, thus depriving over 300,000 citizens of this service. Burundi is one of Africa's poorest countries, with an extremely high rate of illiteracy.

The Catholic press and religious broadcasts were suspended, so the church had no access to the media.

Church-state relations in Burundi had been so bad that in November of 1986 Pope John Paul II sent a letter to the bishops of the country expressing his concern for the difficult situation of the church there. In his letter, the pope specifically mentioned the expulsion of missionaries, the jailing of priests, the suppression of Catholic lay movements, and the nationalization of Catholic schools.

In June of 1987, the government banned weekday Masses in the country in spite of the fact that the population is sixty-five percent Catholic. Lt. Col. Charles Kazatsa, Interior Minister, issued a communique that said, in part, "Many people sacrifice a good part of the workday going to places of worship and return home too late at night." Since 1985, the celebration of Mass before five p.m. had been forbidden.

Then, in November of 1987, Burundi's new government issued new rules restoring freedom of worship, and allowing church-run schools and even permitting the presence of foreign missionaries.

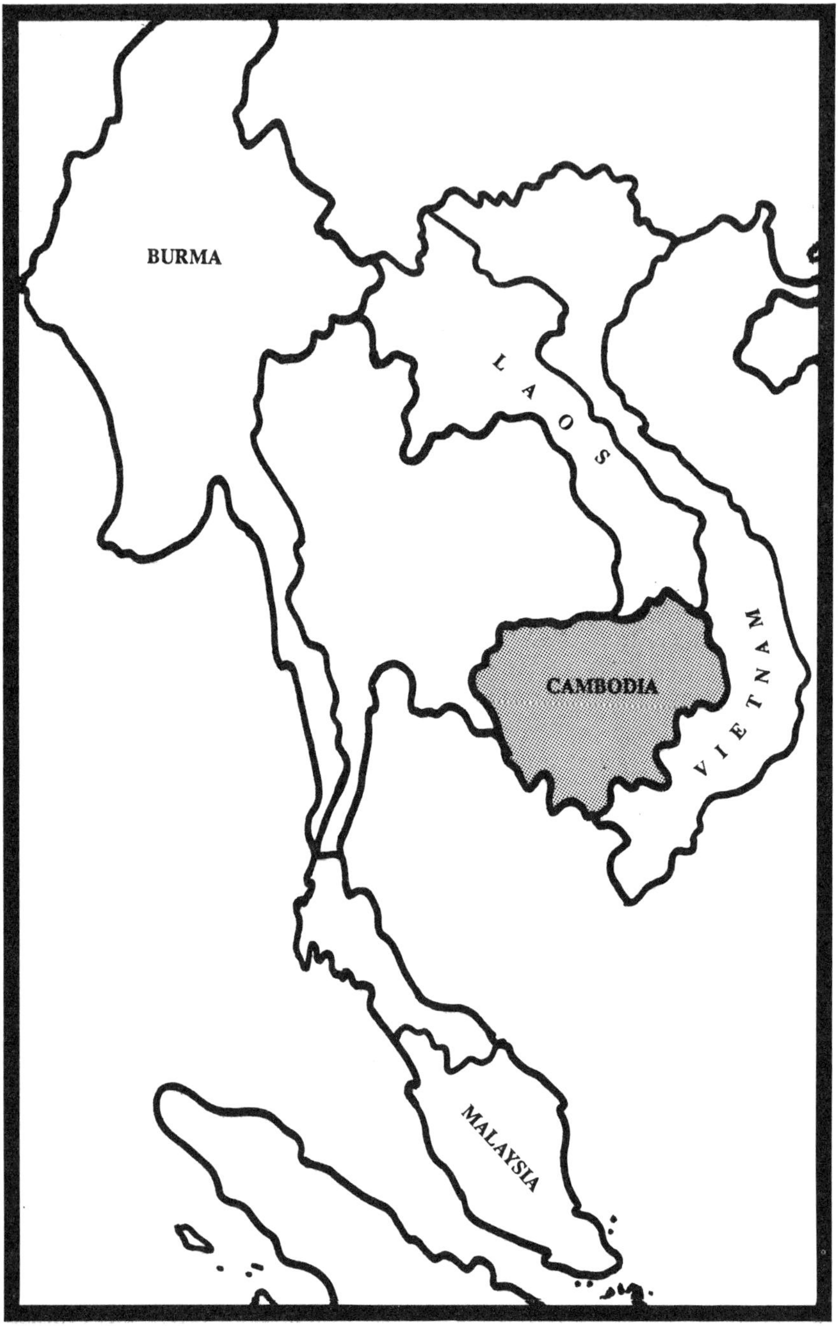
BURMA
LAOS
CAMBODIA
VIETNAM
MALAYSIA

Cambodia

When in power, the Khmer Rouge ruthlessly suppressed Christianity, as well as Islam and Buddhism. In the Khmer Rouge-controlled areas, although there has been a reported lightening of opposition to Buddhism, it is not known if Christianity and Islam have been revived. The Heng Samrin regime has allowed the return of religious practices, but Christian groups are harassed by the regime. Catholic and Protestant communities in Phnom Penh are reportedly not authorized to meet.

In 1988, a Catholic priest was allowed into Cambodia for the first time since 1975: Bishop Guy Derobaix of Saint Denis, France, visited the country as head of a delegation from the French Catholic Committee Against Hunger. He reported that there were still Christians in the country, dispersed, meeting when possible, and that Christian communities were springing up and attracting converts.

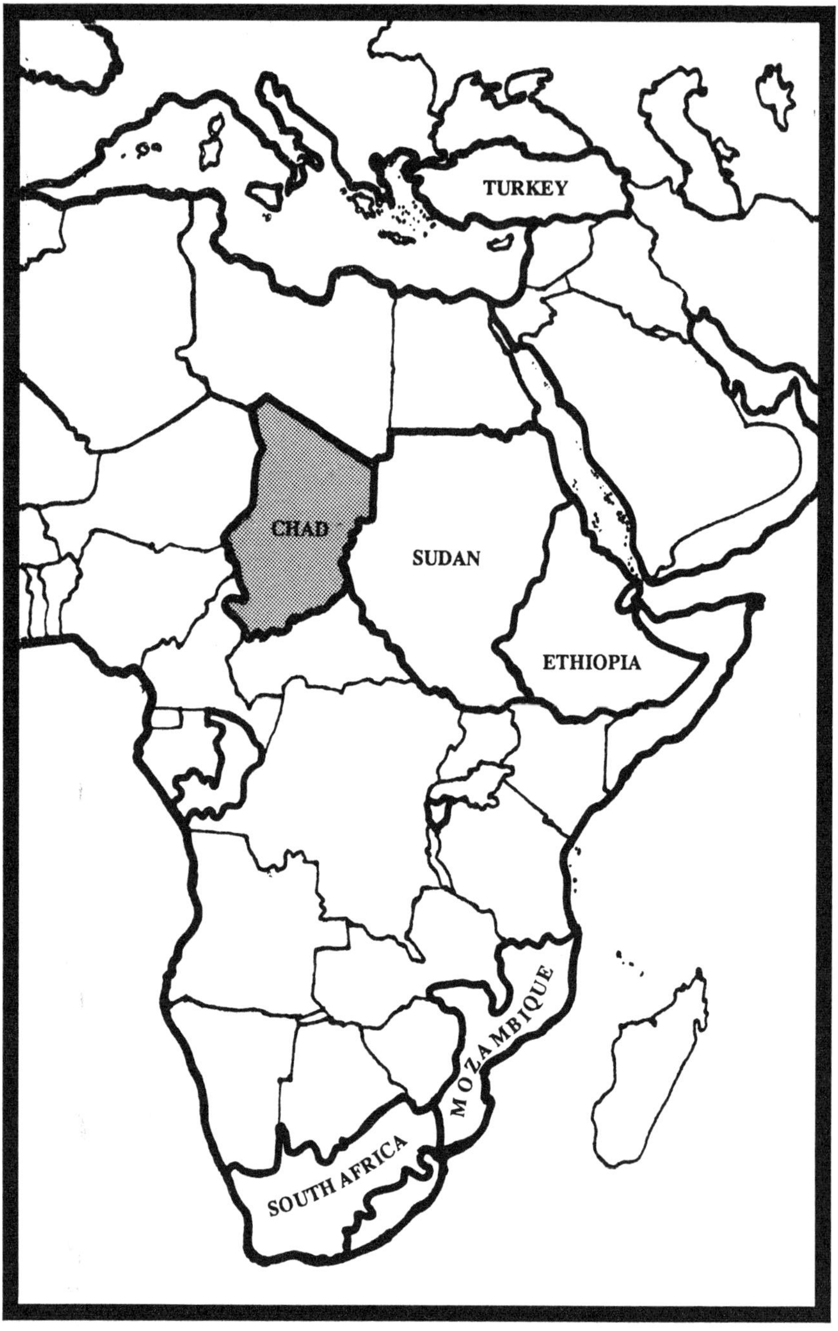
TURKEY
CHAD
SUDAN
ETHIOPIA
MOZAMBIQUE
SOUTH AFRICA

Chad

Chad allows the free practice of religion in the southern part of the country. In Libyan-occupied territory, however, religious practice is limited, in keeping with Qadhafi's avowed mission to spread Islam. In 1986 there were charges that some Catholic priests were working with the insurgents, but no overt action was taken against them.

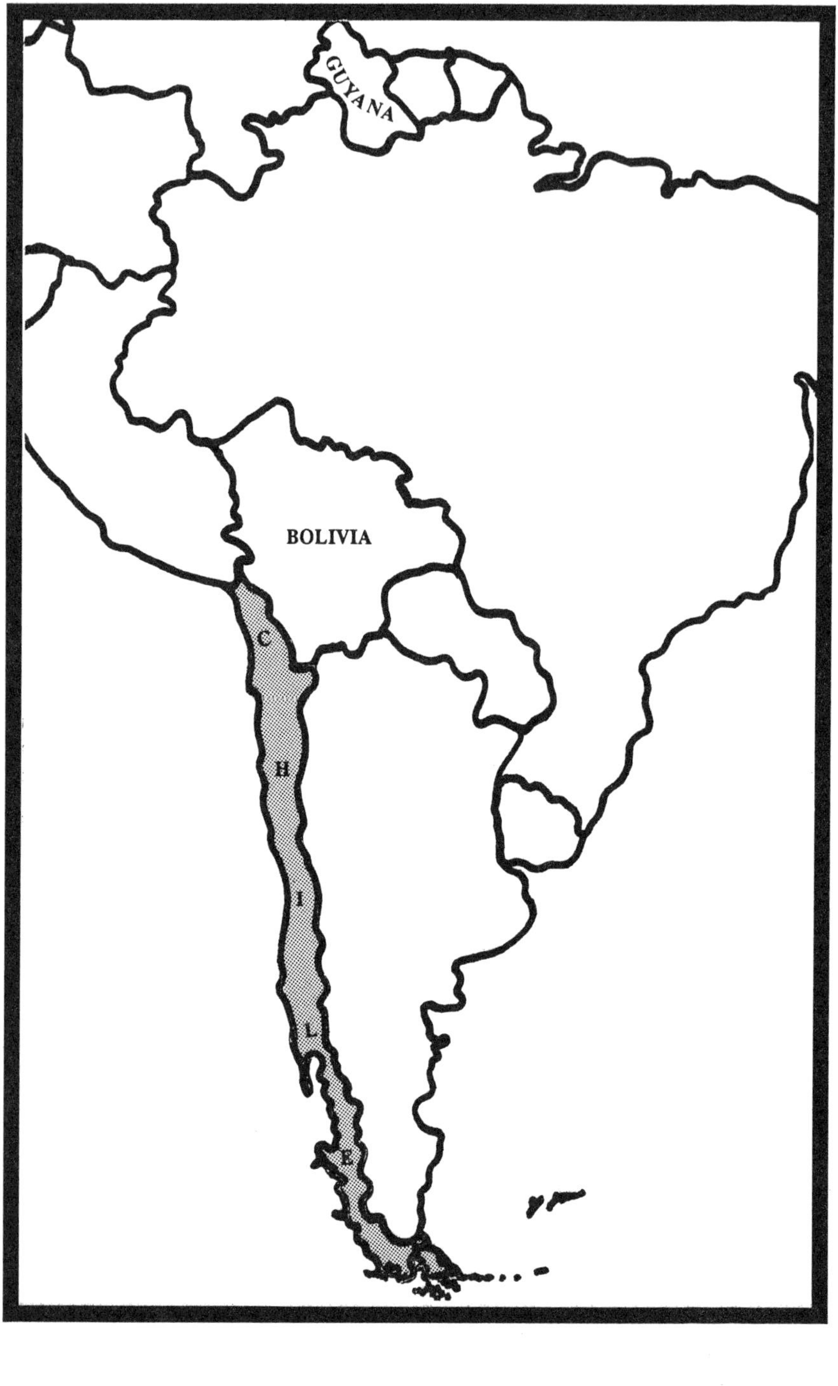
GUYANA
BOLIVIA
C
H
I
L
E

Chile

In spite of the fact that the constitution guarantees absolute freedom of religion, there were at least seventeen bombings against the Mormon church in 1986. Additionally, there were a number of attacks against the officials and the property of the Catholic church. Shots were fired against the Bishops of Osorno and Temuco. The Bishop of Concepcion was threatened. Catholic lay workers are often the victims of threats and intimidation, especially those working in the poorest areas. Some clergymen were briefly detained, and two American priests had their residence permits limited. Three French priests were expelled after government allegations that they were interfering in domestic affairs.

In late 1984, the government prohibited media coverage of a pastoral statement by the Archbishop of Santiago. The statement was regarding the mass police sweeps made in areas of Santiago. The government did not, however, interfere with the church's publication and distribution of the pastoral. During the same month, the archbishop also issued a pastoral letter critical of the government for censorship of the church and for human rights violations. Some church television programs were censored, and the government cancelled a Catholic church's November celebration of the thirteenth annual social week to consider a peaceful transition to democracy in Chile.

Also in late 1984, the government forbade the return to Chile of a Spanish priest who was the head of the Catholic church's human rights organization, the Vicariate of Solidarity. A French priest was shot in his residence during a demonstration in September, but an officer of the Carabinero was charged with his death. A priest from the United States was expelled from the country allegedly for his activities related to a campaign against torture.

The director of the Vicariate of Solidarity, Jose Manuel Parada, was found with his throat slashed in March 1985. A special investigative judge concluded that a police unit was responsible for the killing.

Shortly before Pope John Paul's 1987 visit to Latin America, the Vatican issued a statement on the Third World debt crisis, calling on creditors to adopt an "ethical" approach to alleviating debt burdens. The statement, the pope's visit, and the Vatican policies with regard to Latin America seem to be involving the church even more directly in the region's problems of poverty and repression. In Chile, the church has taken an active role in social reform. It has often focused opposition to Gen. Pinochet, in spite of the fact that in private he is a Catholic communicant.

During the pope's visit to Latin America, he called strongly for people and nations to make "the force of reason prevail over the reasons of force." Borrowing a phrase from a plaque commemorating a Chile-Argentina peace accord, he asked the world to pledge to live in peace until the Andes Mountains crumble.

* * *

On April 3, 1987, at the House of Christ Hospice in Santiago, Pope John Paul II met with "La Quemada" (the burned one).

"I am the girl who was burned, fighting for justice," she told him.

As he hugged her, the pope said, "You don't need to tell me, Carmen Gloria. I know your whole story. Keep up your struggle."

The fire that burned Gloria during a student protest in Chile also burned away her fear. "I've lost all fear," said Carmen Gloria Quintana. "It's made me stronger."

Carmen is the second daughter of six children of an electrician from Santiago. She was part of the Jesuit Holy Cross parish's youth movement, and a student at Santiago University. At the university, she participated in anti-government demonstrations and helped out on Sundays at soup kitchens for the poor. At one of the soup kitchens she met Rodrigo Rojas, a young Chilean who had lived in North America for the past ten years.

Rodrigo's mother had been tortured and raped by Chilean soldiers, and he had returned to Chile to photograph the brutality of the regime.

On July 2, 1986, a two-day strike was to begin in Santiago, accompanied by protests. Carmen, Rodrigo, and some other students and friends planned to build a barricade of used-car tires across the main road in the Nogales zone and set them on fire. Rodrigo was equipped with two cameras to photograph the protest.

Before the barricade could be built, an army truck with soldiers whose faces were blackened with camouflage grease arrived. The soldiers were armed with rifles and submachine guns. The students began to run away, and the soldiers followed. Rodrigo and Carmen were caught. He was questioned, and then battered with the rifle butts and kicked until he lost consciousness. Then Carmen, after identifying herself as a student, was beaten and cursed. Two civilians spoke with the soldiers, then drove off. The lieutenant in charge of the soldiers, Pedro Fernandez, poured gasoline over Rodrigo and Carmen and ignited it. About twenty witnesses at a nearby bus stop watched, but did not interfere or attempt to help. Carmen attempted to beat out the flames, but blacked out.

The next thing she was aware of was Rodrigo tapping her legs. She smelled the stench of burnt flesh, which she realized was from her own as well as Rodrigo's body. The pair had been wrapped in blankets and taken about eight miles toward the airport and dumped in a ditch. The previous year, three beheaded corpses of opponents of the regime had been found near the same place.

Carmen and Rodrigo dragged themselves from the ditch and staggered to the highway. A worker called the military police, who called an ambulance that never arrived. Finally after about two hours a van took them to a hospital. Rodrigo died four days later. The Canadian Catholic Development and Peace Organization arranged the transfer of Carmen and seven of her family to Montreal, where she continued to receive treatment for her burns.

Carmen suffered third-degree burns on fifty percent of her body. After 1,200 E-rays and sixteen skin grafts, she was still due for more treatment. Her lips have been reconstructed, but her mouth still needed widening, and she needed dental work because her front teeth had been knocked out, probably by a rifle butt. She had lost one ear, but her hair had grown in again. Much of her body had to be encased in elasticized garments to help the skin grow close to normal.

The Chilean Catholic human rights watchdog organization, the Vicariate of Solidarity, took up the case. Protests were so large that the government took action against the soldiers, but all charges were dropped except those against Lt. Fernandez. He was to be tried before a military court for "unnecessary violence."

Carmen has become a human torch for justice. She told her story in early 1987 to the United Nations Human Rights Commission in Geneva. The publicity surrounding the case of this courageous Catholic human rights activist is pointing out to the world that human rights are still denied to many in Chile.

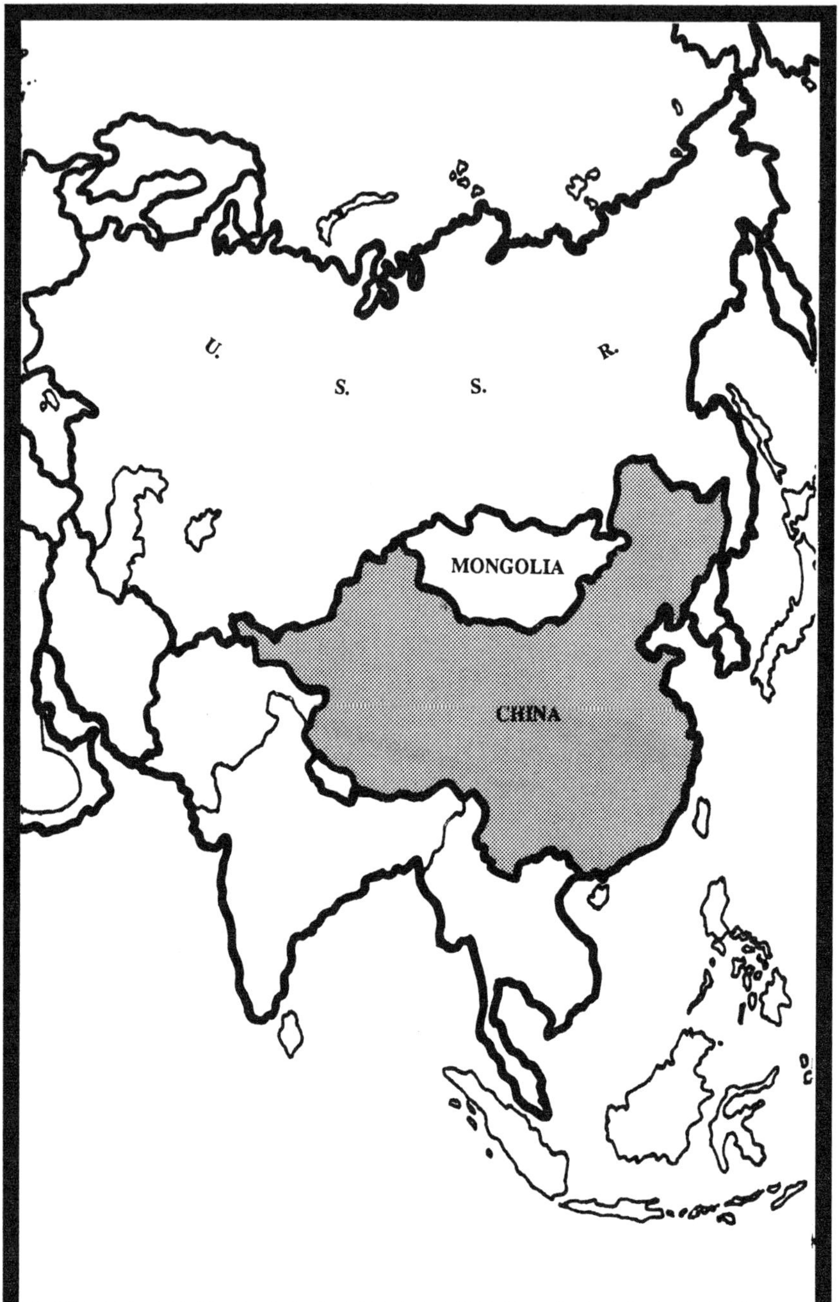
U.
S.
S.
R.
MONGOLIA
CHINA

China

In 1978, China's reformist leadership instituted a policy of limited tolerance of religion. The Cultural Revolution's attempts to completely eliminate all religious practices simply had not worked. There are certain constitutional guarantees for religion, but there is also a provision that religious groups must not be subject to foreign domination. Obviously, this provision directly affects the Roman Catholic church. Official policy prohibits proselytizing outside of designated places of worship and believers' homes.

Officially, all churches in China are required to be affiliated with eight national organizations. These associations have differing functional responsibilities and overlapping leaderships, and link the religious groups to the state and the Communist Party. They constitute the officially sanctioned national church. Four religions are recognized: Christianity, Buddhism, Islam, and Daoism.

The Protestant Three-Self Movement and the China Christian Council are the Protestant groups. Since the 1950's, all Protestant churches in China have been merged, although they may still follow individual preferences in matters such as which form of baptism to use.

The Patriotic Catholic Association, the National Administrative Council of the Catholic church, and the Catholic Bishops' College are the Catholic groups. Since being separated from Rome thirty years ago, the Chinese Catholic church has developed an independent theology and doctrines. Some major points are its rejection of papal supremacy and infallibility and its support of the state's policy on birth control, provided church-approved methods are used. Additionally, the Chinese Catholic church conducts services in Latin. The Catholic Patriotic Association is not recognized by the Vatican. It is often used for propaganda purposes and much of the Catholic population of the country ignores it.

Over the last few years, there has been a gradual resumption of many religious practices, and many religious institutions that had been closed since the Cultural Revolution have reopened. In 1986, officials announced that there were over 30,000 buildings of worship in use.

Beginning in 1981, the government allowed a limited number of seminaries to begin operation. The Catholic Church has ten seminaries, and the Protestants operate one national seminary and nine theological institutes. A variety of religious publications are allowed. The Protestant China Christian Council reported that since 1980 it has printed and distributed over 1.3 million Bibles. Since 1987 the Chinese government has allowed the Amity Printing Company in Nanjing to print Bibles and hymnbooks.

Estimates of the number of Christians in China range from 6 million to 20 million. There is a great shortage of religious leaders, and of buildings of worship. Thus, many congregations meet in believers' homes.

In spite of the increased freedom in recent years, the government still reacts harshly against officially unsanctioned religious activity. Some Christians disagree with the "patriotic" church, and meet clandestinely in homes. These underground churches are harassed by public security authorities. In May of 1986, an unofficial Catholic seminary in Hebei province was raided, and forty Catholics were arrested. Some of these were later released. In June, four Catholic seminarians were arrested in the same area.

In 1983, there were a number of reports of arrests of church members and leaders. Thirty "house church" leaders were arrested in Central China; a hundred Christians were jailed in Henan Province, and two Evangelicals were jailed in Shanghai. In the months following the June 1988 massacre of protesting students in Tiananmen Square, the communist government began a new crackdown on the Roman Catholic Church, arresting more than thirty-five priests and bishops.

Although Chinese religious leaders are encouraged to meet foreign counterparts, these meetings are carefully monitored. In 1986, Hong Kong's Roman Catholic Bishop John Baptist Wu and South African Bishop Desmond Tutu were allowed to visit China. A group of Chinese Catholic leaders was allowed to accept an invitation by the association of Catholic Colleges and Universities to visit the United States.

The Chinese government has not relaxed its strict injunction against foreign control of or influence on religion and prohibits missionaries from practicing among Chinese citizens. Some foreign clergymen have been allowed to enter the country for brief times to serve the resident foreign community. In particular, the Chinese government targets the Vatican as a source of foreign interference, partially because the Vatican has retained diplomatic ties with Taiwan. Any Chinese priest who publicly maintains loyalty to the pope is subject to arrest and imprisonment.

The organization Free the Fathers reports that there are as many as one hundred Catholic priests in their seventies and eighties who are still in prison or in forced-labor camps after thirty years. In these camps, they quarry rock, work in steel smelters or labor in rice paddies. Some of these priests are tortured.

Until 1985, Bishop Ignatius Kung, now in his eighties, was being kept in solitary confinement. He then was moved from prison to house arrest, and in 1988 was paroled and allowed to move to the United States. Father Joseph Chen, S.J., age seventy-eight, was being kept in handcuffs twenty-four hours a day in

Shanghai's No. 1 Prison. Many priests, such as Father Thomas Tao and Father Francis Chu, have died in prison. In 1984, Bishop Peter Fan, age seventy-seven, of the Diocese of Baoding, was sentenced to an additional ten years in prison. Free the Fathers also reported that hundreds of "house church" leaders, primarily Baptists, Pentecostals and Presbyterians, have also been arrested and jailed.

In April 1989, Chinese police raided the village of Youtong, where Catholics had been having Mass outdoors under a tent. About 5,000 policemen were employed in the raid on the village, which was home to 1,700 Catholics. Two people were killed and hundreds injured, and hospitals were forbidden to treat the injured.

* * *

In 1949, Father Francis Xavier Chu Shu-Teh, S.J., wrote to his brother Michael: "Every day, there are a lot of people escaping from mainland China to Hong Kong. I think that one can hardly find another one except myself who wants to leave Hong Kong and return to the mainland. Some say that I am a fool! It is quite true that according to the viewpoint of this world, I am really a first-class fool! When businessmen find that a place is useless for trade, they go elsewhere. But I am a priest and priests must live for their people. As long as there are Catholics in Shanghai, I must return there; even if there were only one Catholic, or if there were no more Catholics in Shanghai, I would still have to go back because I am a priest, a representative of Christ and of His Church. Where I am, there the Church is. I am willing to be in Shanghai and remain there to let the Communists know that the Catholic Church still exists in mainland China."

For over thirty years, Father Francis existed in mainland China, in silent martyrdom and persecution in labor camp and prison, living proof that the Catholic church does indeed exist in mainland China.

Francis Chu Shu-Teh was born in 1913, the oldest of nine children of a devoutly Catholic family. The Christian influence of his grandmother and both of his parents had great impact on the formation of his own beliefs. One of his brothers stated that "faith is the most precious heritage of the Chu family." Another of his brothers also grew up to become a Jesuit, and four of his brothers attempted to follow God's call to the priesthood although due to the difficult circumstances some have not yet succeeded in realizing their desire.

Francis entered the Society of Jesus in 1935 and was ordained in 1945 in Shanghai. He received his Ph.D. from the Sorbonne in 1949.

In 1949, after a brief stay in Hong Kong, Father Francis returned to Shanghai, where he was appointed professor at Aurora University and spiritual director of the Catholic students. Here he organized the students into small groups for catechetical studies, as religious studies had been removed from the regular curriculum. These groups deepened the students' Catholic faith, preparing them for the harsh times to come.

In 1951, the government took over the university, and Father Francis became pastor of the parish of Christ the King in Shanghai. Here, Father Francis continued the same tireless apostolic activity that had characterized his time at the university. He maintained his contact with the students and their study groups. Sometimes his parishioners would urge him to rest, but he would reply, "I still have some sheep to take care of—if even one of them is in need, I cannot rest."

By 1953, all places of education had been taken over by the state, and foreign missionaries had been through accusation meetings before finally being imprisoned or expelled from the country. In his last letter before arrest, Father Francis wrote to his younger brother on the eve of Michael's ordination, "I will be closely united with you in your first Sacrifice of the Mass. But God willing, I will unite with you in another kind of sacrifice. May I always be at God's disposal."

On June 15, 1953, armed policemen showed up at Father

Francis's room in Christ the King church. During their search of his possessions, they found some handbooks from the Legion of Mary, which had been listed as a counter-revolutionary organization. Father Francis was arrested that night, as were many other priests in the diocese of Shanghai.

Three days after his arrest, one of his brothers wrote, "Two days ago, our elder brother started his way of the cross with Christ. Please pray for him in union with us, with one heart and one mind. Also let us thank the good God with one voice because He has visited our family in a special way and has chosen one among us to bear witness to Him."

It was not until March 12, 1960, that Father Francis was formally sentenced to twenty years' imprisonment—seven years after his arrest!

Father Francis was sentenced to White Lake Camp in Anhui province. This labor camp is a cheap slave-labor camp populated by about 20,000 prisoners. A number of other Jesuits and priests were detained there. These "criminals" of all types were given "productive" tasks, primarily agricultural and factory work. When Father Francis was first sentenced and carried to the camp, he was forty years old. He and his fellow priests offered a total sacrifice, expressing their faith and love in the form of selfless service in the prison camps.

After long hours of work, there was still no rest on their return at night. The prisoners then had several hours of political indoctrination, and the dreaded accusation meetings with self-accusations exacted and constant psychological pressure, all within an environment of fear, threat, suspicion and hatred. Sometimes the guards encouraged the prisoners to physically beat and abuse other prisoners.

These priests, however, did not waste time in self-pity. They put themselves at the service of others who were suffering in the same situation.

During the years 1959-1961, an estimated 12 million to 24

million Chinese died from starvation. Food was even scarcer in the labor camps than for the common people, and many died daily in the camps. Father Aloysius Wong Jen-Shen, S.J., was one among the many who died at that time. Father Francis was happy to assist him at the time of his death. On his deathbed, Father Wong repeated these words of St. Paul: "I have fought the good fight, I have finished the race, and I have redeemed my pledge; I look forward to the prize that is waiting for me, the prize I have earned." A pagan who was in the same camp and who eventually was released gave witness to the good example Father Wong had given to everyone. He himself was so inspired by Father Wong's example that he asked to be baptized secretly.

By the end of Father Francis' sentence, he was over sixty and in poor health. He was detained an additional two years in camp, and twenty-two years after his captivity had begun he made his first visit home.

After a brief and joyful reunion, he, along with his brothers, was re-arrested and returned to the labor camp. On his return to camp, his active apostolate among his fellow prisoners continued. It also extended to the wider circle of his family and friends to whom, in one letter, he wrote, "Be fervent. Put yourself in the hands of God. Let His will be done. There are crosses everywhere, not only in China. Bear your cross willingly and follow Jesus Christ."

In 1977, Father Francis suffered from hepatitis and a problem with his gall bladder. He went to Shanghai for a medical consultation and on his return he was assigned to lighter works and chores. He never complained, and never lost his keen sense of humor. In one letter he wrote, "By Cistercian standards, our life here is not too austere nor are we living in too great solitude." One time when he was scolded by the cadre for his slow output, he remarked, "I am not slow—my pace is normal. It's just that the others are too quick."

Father Francis was an example to many in the camp—he was

brave, cheerful, caring about others and never seeming to care about himself. He said, "We people inside under oppression are not afraid of spreading God's Kingdom—then why should you people outside be afraid? Of course, we have to be prudent and wise, but not timid. We must try our best to avoid unnecessary trouble—on the alert as a snake is. But, if necessary, I'm willing to fight to the death for my Faith. I am not concerned about money, position, power ... I want only to do everything for the glory of God."

In the hostile environment of the labor camp, Father Francis helped, encouraged, instructed and baptized those who asked his help. For him it was a joy to accept and follow the one Who Himself was "obedient unto death."

During his last year in labor camp, Father Francis lived alone in a small hut. Here he rejoiced to have the freedom to write articles on many religious subjects and to translate papal addresses that were sent to him. He wrote, "Put yourself in the hands of God. Let His will be done. Bear your cross willingly and follow Jesus Christ." Through his own suffering, he had a deep understanding of its value. "There are many just people who have met discrimination, hostility, imprisonment, exile ... Has life any meaning and value for them? When we contemplate Jesus in His sufferings, willing to suffer still more for me, then if I can suffer for Him in return, I should feel glad and honored just like the disciples who after being scourged were 'happy because God had considered them worthy to suffer disgrace for the name of Jesus.' "

Father Francis was allowed short visits home in 1979 and 1980. In November 1981, he was arrested in the labor camp and sent from camp to prison on the same day. After that, all communications were cut off. According to a reliable report, he was tried and sentenced to twelve years' imprisonment.

On December 27, 1983, a relative visited Father Francis in prison at Ho Fei in Anhui Province. Early the next morning, Father Francis had a heart attack and died within a few hours, at the age of seventy-one.

On March 9, 1983, a solemn Mass was held in Kowloon to commemorate the death of this modern martyr. Archbishop Tang gave the homily. It was a moving occasion for him as he, too, had been imprisoned for over twenty years. These words of Father Francis were read: "If we do not carry the Cross, we cannot arrive at a true understanding of the Church nor be a true disciple of Christ."

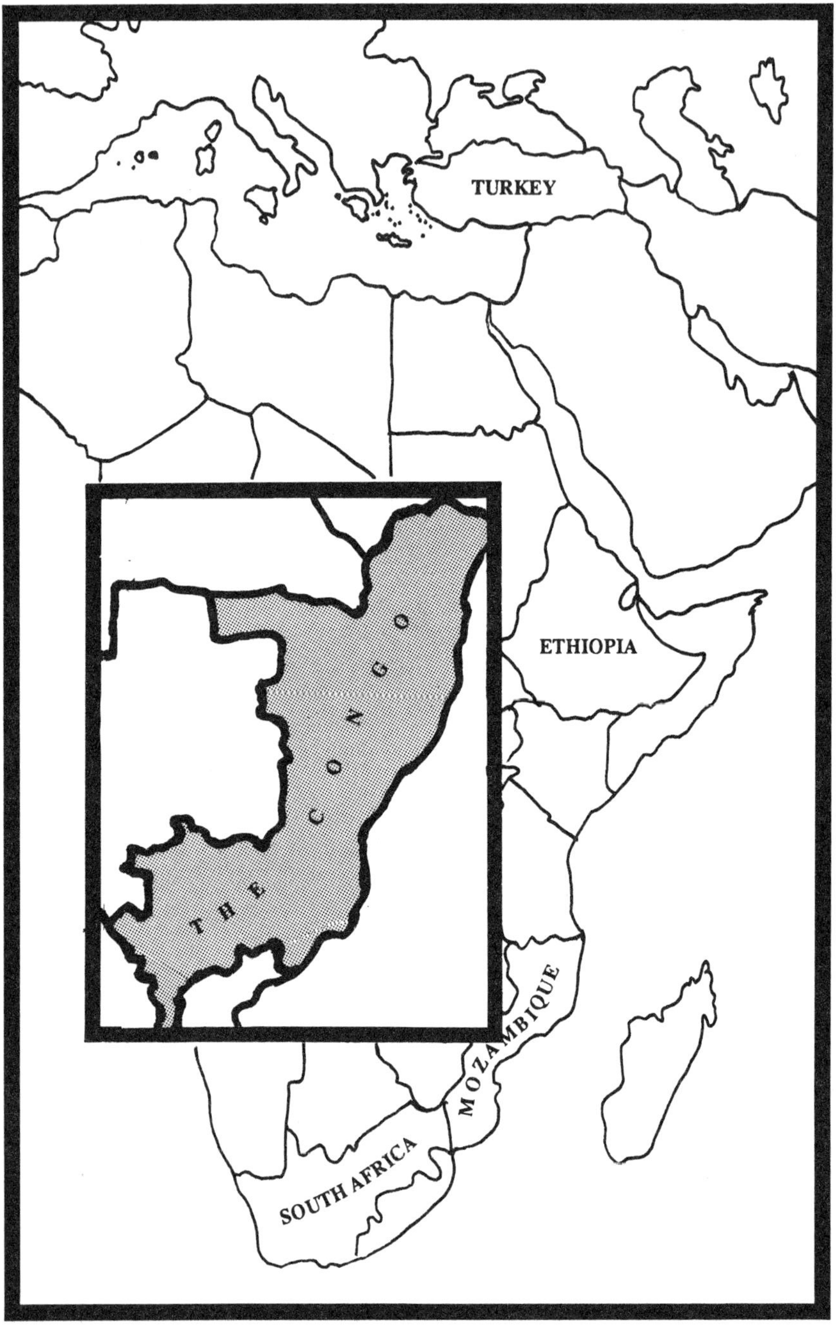
TURKEY
ETHIOPIA
THE CONGO
MOZAMBIQUE
SOUTH AFRICA

The Congo

The People's Republic of the Congo is officially an atheist state. Religious freedom is guaranteed by law; in fact, however, party members are prohibited from practicing any religion. All religious organizations, churches and charitable groups must have permission to work in the country. Just as in many other countries, the Jehovah's Witness sect is forbidden due to their refusal to recognize the authority of the state. With this exception, the party does not normally interfere with the practice of religion in the country. The Catholic church is the largest congregation and it and other denominations run missions and social service works throughout the Congo. The Catholics operate a seminary and publish the only non-government newspaper. The churches cooperate with the government on some projects for social services, although in recent years many services formerly operated by the church have been abolished.

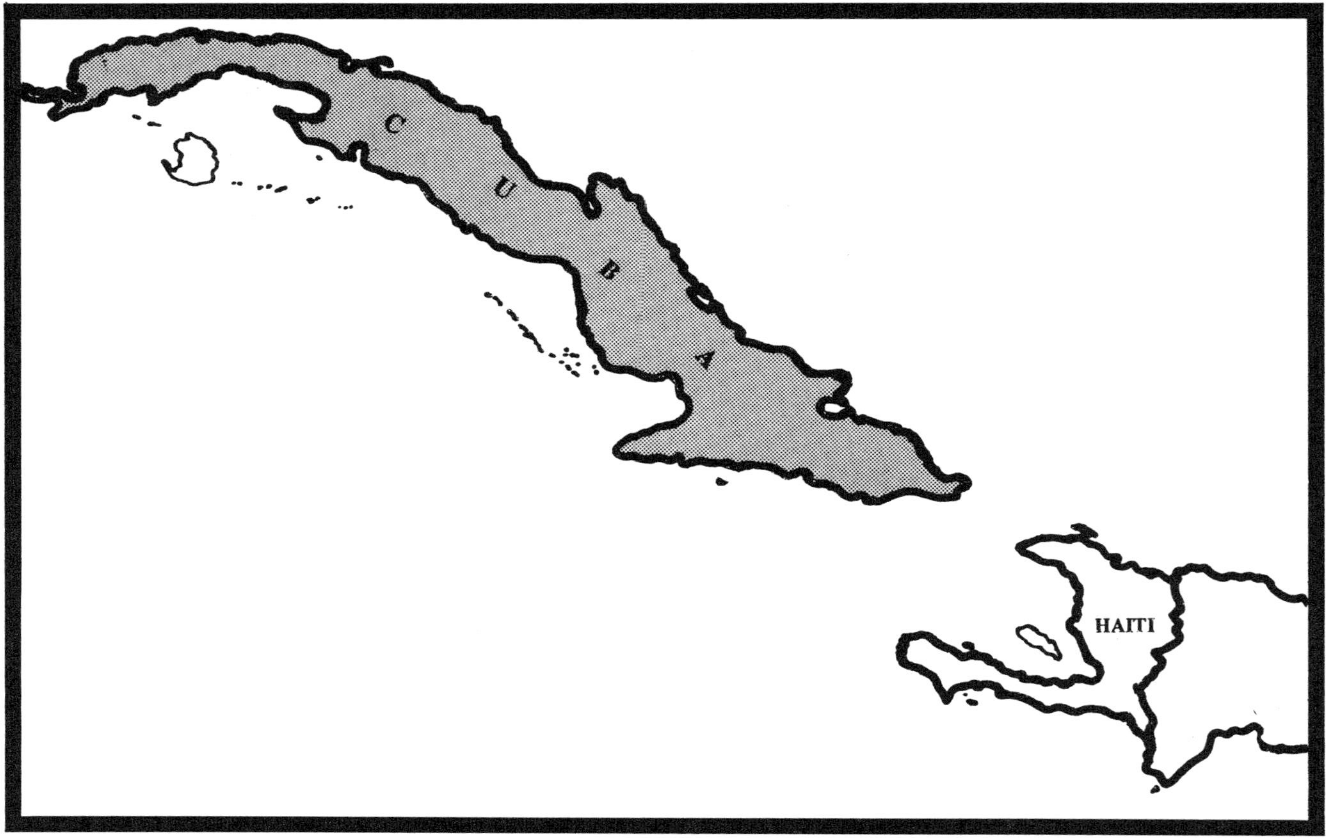
CUBA
HAITI

Cuba

In 1985, Cuba established a Religious Affairs Office of the Central Committee of the Communist party to administer church-state relations. For the first time in twenty years, the government allowed the Catholic church to hold a national conference in 1986. Additionally, Mother Teresa of Calcutta was allowed to establish a small branch of her order with four sisters in Havana. At the request of the United States Catholic Conference, Castro agreed to release a group of over three hundred political prisoners beginning in September of 1987.

In spite of the moderate signs of official tolerance, Cubans who openly practice their religion face serious discrimination. Membership in the Cuban Communist Party is still required in order to hold important positions in the government, and for advancement in many fields, making these things difficult for those who openly profess religious faith.

Religious groups must register with the government, and religious materials are not allowed to circulate freely. Although four Protestant and two Catholic seminaries are allowed to operate, religious elementary schools, secondary schools, and colleges are prohibited. The church has virtually no access to the press.

Long-standing government practices discouraging religion have taken their toll, and the majority of Cuban worshipers are over fifty. Even in their homes, families rightly fear that teaching their children religious practices will hold them back in their chosen careers.

All activity at the few neighborhood churches that are still open is monitored. This causes many to attend the larger downtown churches in hopes that they will be less obvious. One law prohibits religious ceremonies outside of church walls. Children who admit going to church are held up for ridicule by their classmates, and active involvement in the communist youth organization is strongly encouraged. Castro has openly admitted discrimination against those who practice their religious beliefs. Recently, however, the government seems to be relaxing somewhat in order to convince the religious believers to go along with some of the government policies and to publicly proclaim their agreement with these policies. In a book published in 1985, *Fidel and Religion*, Castro appeared to view Christianity as useful for revolution. Castro insisted that priests were never tortured or murdered, and that Cuba had never closed a single church. (From 1961 on, however, the churches in Cuba were repressed. Priests were exiled and jailed and all religious schools were nationalized. Hundreds of priests and thousands of religious were either expelled or left the country in fear of reprisals from the regime.)

A number of observers believe that two things are contributing to Castro's detente with religious leaders: first, the relative weakness of religion in Cuba today, and, second, the fact that the government has realized that it is counterproductive to persecute religious believers, since persecution generates sympathy for the believers.

* * *

On Sunday, April 5, 1987, four native Cuban priests and a Spanish-born priest raised the sacred host in concelebration of a Mass for Cuban political prisoners. The Mass was said at Sacred Heart Co-cathedral in Houston, Texas. The Spanish-born priest, Father Feliciano del Val, had been invited to join the celebration because of his many years of devoted service in Cuba, and his experience of political imprisonment there.

Over fifty years ago, shortly after his ordination, Father del Val, a Dominican, left his convent in Ciudad Real, Spain, for his order's mission in Cuba. The young priest left obediently, but with a heavy heart, for he would have preferred to stay teaching in Spain. His obedience probably saved his life. As the ship entered tropical waters, news came of the outbreak of the Spanish Civil War.

Father Feliciano's convent was taken by the reds and every Dominican over twenty-one was killed. His former superior was literally cut into small pieces. The younger men were imprisoned with the thought of re-educating them, but few of them survived the bloody three-year conflict.

For the next twenty-five years, Father Feliciano labored in the mission fields of Cuba. He worked in the parish of San Juan de Letran in Havana, and in a slum area of the city called Pan con Timba. He worked as a teacher, and in mission works in the provinces. His work at one of these missions took him to the infamous penitentiary on the Isle of the Pines.

Within months of strongman Fidel Castro's entry into Havana in 1959, the church began to endure persecution and attacks from the government-controlled communications media. Castro's revolutionary government had begun a period of active anti-religious activity aimed at eradicating believers.

On April 7, 1961, Father Feliciano returned to his convent to find it occupied by armed militia. He was escorted to a small upstairs sitting room. In company with the other seventeen Dominicans who lived there, he spent days in that one room, sleeping on the floor. The militia threatened them with guns if they dared get near a window, and provided guards even in the bathroom. Finally, they were allowed to go to their own rooms at night. One night Father Feliciano was wakened by a guard and pushed into a hallway, where all of the residents of the house were lined up against a wall. They feared that they were about to be executed.

Father del Val was singled out and told that he had been accused by a woman of being counter-revolutionary. He was then taken by jeep to the G-Dos headquarters. He was accused of spying for the Americans because he owned a ham radio receiver. He was interrogated for hours, and threats and promises were made. At last, he was escorted to a small cell, which he shared for a week with thirty other prisoners.

Father del Val later recalled that there was not enough room to lie down and that the prisoners had to take turns in order to sleep. "Our daily ration of food consisted of a small box of boiled rice. Aside from this, two or three times a day a five-ounce Coca Cola bottle filled with water was brought to us by our jailers. As we passed it around, there was barely enough for each of us to wet our lips." Here, in this crowded cell, Father del Val spent the day of his silver anniversary of ordination to the priesthood.

After about a week, Father del Val was sent to the Teatro Blanquita, a theater that had been turned into a jail for about 5,000 alleged counter-revolutionaries. He was jailed here for nearly a month, with very little food and almost no sanitary facilities.

"Human refuse was knee deep in the bathrooms. We were afraid an epidemic would break out. Once in a while they washed down the place with fire hoses, demolishing everything and causing rivers of filthy water down the aisles." In recalling the reactions of his fellow inmates, Father Feliciano said that "Some cried, others uttered obscenities, some prayed, some sat in a daze. From the balconies where the women were, screams of terror resounded once in a while." At night, there was shooting in the attic, intended to convince the prisoners that there were executions taking place.

Finally, a mock revolutionary tribunal began to set people free. Father Feliciano still has the form he was issued at his release. The form is blank except for the signature. There are no dates or accusations on it. Father said, "They were too lazy to fill it out."

Within three months, Father Feliciano was the only priest left at the San Juan de Letran convent. The others had left the country. One day in September, armed militia came to the convent and ordered Father del Val to pack for a long journey. Suspecting that it was a journey to his death, Father only took a shirt and a pair of sandals. Instead, his trip ended at the Port of Havana, where he was herded along with about three hundred other priests and religious onto a crowded Spanish ship. The exit document he was given at the time reads: "By courtesy of the Revolutionary Government of Cuba."

For more than twenty-five years, Father del Val has served in the diocese of Galveston-Houston. At the Mass for Cuban political prisoners, Father del Val stood as one who understands the condition of prisoners of conscience in Cuba, and in other parts of the world. He knows. He was there.

ESTONIA
LATVIA
LITHUANIA
GERMAN DEMOCRATIC REPUBLIC
POLAND
CZECHOSLOVAKIA
HUNGARY
ROMANIA
YUGOSLAVIA
BULGARIA

Czechoslovakia

In spite of constitutional guarantees, religious freedom has been severely limited in Czechoslovakia. The regime has espoused "scientific atheism" and discouraged all forms of religious practice. Severe career setbacks have been encountered in many professions for those considered believers, and higher education is often denied to believers and their families.

No new Catholic church buildings have been approved for many years, although a few Protestant congregations have been allowed to build new churches. All churches have been required to register with the state, and the government has exercised strict control over them. Some sects, especially those that proselytize, have been banned, and members imprisoned. Both written and unwritten restrictions have hampered religion. Clergymen have been required to have a license issued by the government (the government also has paid their salary), and these licenses have often been revoked for no discernible reason. If a license has been revoked and the clergyman has still continued to practice, he has been subject to criminal prosecution. In 1986, Stefan Javorsky, a sixty-two-year-old Salesian, was sentenced to twelve months in prison for celebrating private Masses and hearing confessions without state permission. Additionally, he was ordered to undergo psychiatric examination. Father Javorsky had previously been sentenced in 1975 and 1981. Another priest, Bystrik Janik, was sentenced to twenty-eight months in prison for religious activities without a proper permit. An Evangelical minister, Milos Reichert, complained of police harassment, which included confiscation of copies of religious books.

Travel of religious figures into and out of the country has sporadically been approved, especially when it has suited the purposes of the government. The authorities have been severely restrictive of the Catholic church, and the pope has not been permitted to visit in spite of petitions from thousands of Czech and Slovak Catholics. Unofficial travel of religious personnel and the importing of religious materials and objects have been severely punished.

On October 1, 1987, in a talk with Cardinal Tomasek of Prague, Pope John Paul II said that the government's restrictions are "without parallel" in traditionally Catholic countries. The Czech authorities had refused to allow the country's four other active bishops to join the cardinal for their "ad limina" visits to the Vatican, which are normally made by heads of dioceses every five years.

With approximately 8 million to 11 million Roman Catholics, and approximately 450,000 members of the affiliated Greek Uniate church, the Catholic church is the largest of the eighteen officially registered denominations. The Greek Catholics were forcibly united with the Orthodox church in 1950, and only reestablished separately in 1968. This group, however, has not been able to reclaim their property, which remains in possession of the Orthodox church.

In 1950, all male religious orders were dissolved, and although a few female orders were allowed to continue, they were prevented from accepting new members except for a brief time in the late sixties. When the orders were suppressed, many of the members were jailed or forced into hard labor. Some of the monastic orders have continued to operate underground. In June of 1987, reports in the West German Catholic press stated that the Czechoslovakian authorities were cracking down on women illegally joining Catholic religious orders. Communities suspected of admitting new members illegally have been raided by secret police. In recent years, a number of small underground convents and cloisters reportedly have sprung up throughout the country. Men and women who on the surface seem to live conventional lifestyles secretly follow the vows of their particular religious orders. These secret orders made headlines in 1983 when the police raided a number of clandestine Franciscan communities.

There are only two seminaries, and applicants have had to receive state approval for entrance and ordination, as well as pastoral assignments and promotions. As a result of these restrictions, only three of the thirteen dioceses have resident bishops, and many pastors serve more than a single parish. The Vatican has negotiated unsuccessfully for years with Czechoslovakia for the right to name bishops for the other dioceses. The only legally published Catholic newspaper is under the control of priests associated with the government-sponsored association of clergy, an association rejected by Cardinal Tomasek and the majority of the Catholic clergy.

Bibles and other religious literature have been in short supply. Smuggling of these types of materials, and samizdat (self-published) underground activities have been dealt with harshly. Maria Kotrisova was sentenced in 1986 to ten months in prison and Michal Mrtvy recently faced trial for such activities.

Protestant denominations face the same harassment and government restrictions and persecutions as do their Catholic counterparts.

In 1983, the World Psychiatric Association accused Czechoslovakia of misusing psychiatry for political purposes. Czechoslovakia immediately withdrew from the organization. Reports involving cases of this misuse of psychiatry continue to be smuggled out of the country, and the reports are credible. Augustine Navratil, a religious activist, was detained in November of 1985 for distributing samizdat Catholic literature. In December he was sent to a closed psychiatric facility in Prague and moved in March to an institution in Kromeriz. He was not released to ambulatory treatment until October of 1986, and this decision is susceptible to reversal.

The decades since the communist takeover have been a bleak time for Christians. With the political changes taking place in Czechoslovakia, however, it is quite possible that the churches will have their freedom restored.

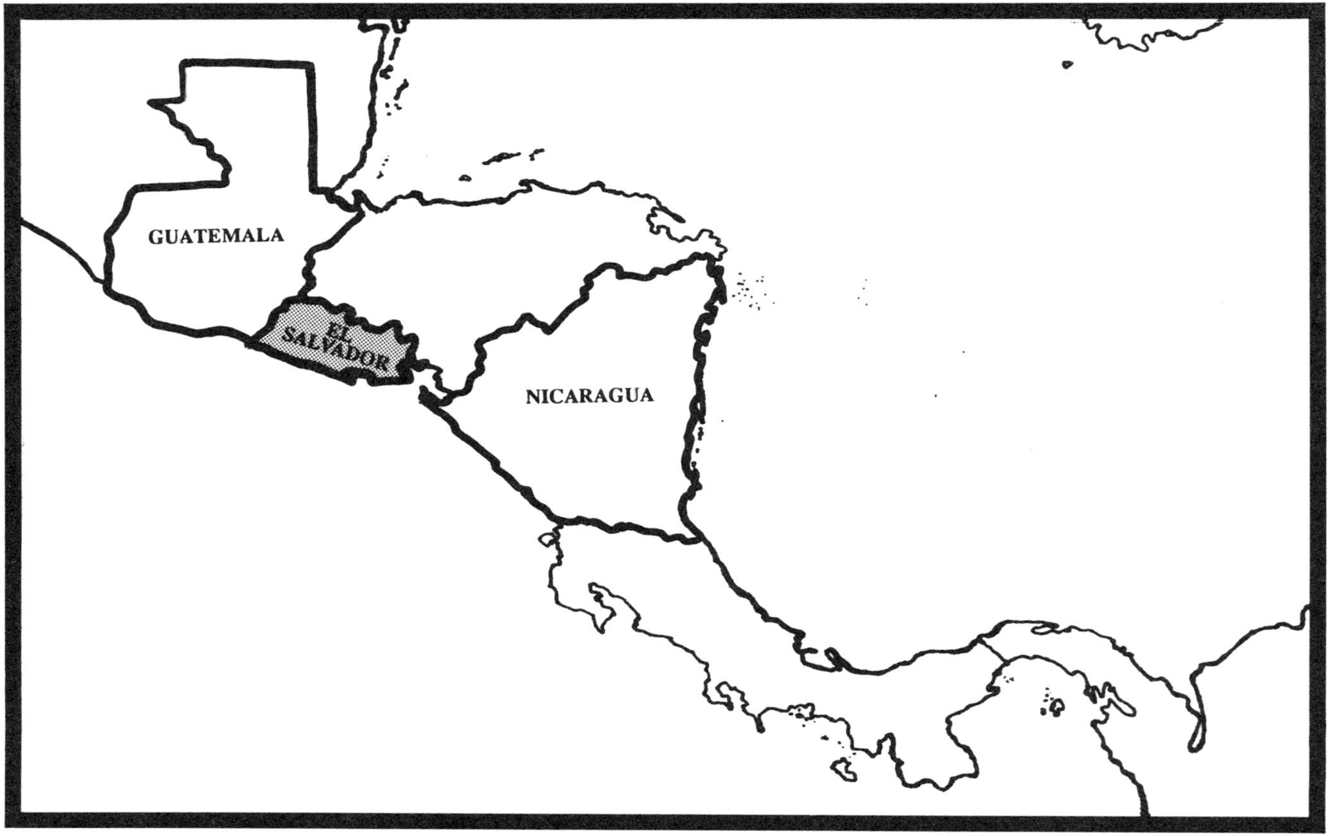
GUATEMALA
EL SALVADOR
NICARAGUA

El Salvador

In El Salvador, freedom of religion is guaranteed by the constitution and is, in many ways, respected in practice. The Catholic church is one of the most influential institutions in the country and the archbishop's Sunday homily is broadcast on government television and on radio. Church publications disseminate the church's position on human rights and the war. Although church statements have become increasingly critical of the leftist insurgency, the church has not hesitated to criticize the government.

But El Salvador, like much of Central America, is a trouble spot. According to Dr. David Barrett, there have been scores of bishops, priests, and other Catholic workers killed throughout Central America in the waves of mindless killing there. He did not feel that here Catholics were targets especially because of their beliefs, but rather because they are working in the trouble spots. Whenever the church speaks out in defense of human rights, there is potential for Christian martyrdom.

Dr. Barrett cited the case of Archbishop Oscar Arnulfo Romero, who was assassinated in 1980 after receiving death threats for criticizing human rights violations. Archbishop Romero was saying Mass in the chapel of Divine Providence Hospital in San Salvador when armed gunmen stood at the back of the church and machine-gunned him.

In 1986, a number of anonymous death threats were publicized. The Archdiocese of San Salvador received a telephoned threat against several of its workers. A Lutheran minister received similar threats following public accusations by guerilla defectors that church workers were diverting humanitarian aid to the guerillas. So many civilians have been seriously injured by mines that the archbishop has expressed grave concern.

In spite of the fact that the Catholic church has taken a courageous role in moderating dialog between the government and guerilla forces, the left and elements of the far right have attacked the church and the auxiliary bishop personally for alleged bias.

* * *

On December 3, 1980, the parish priest of Chalatenango, El Salvador, received a letter. The letter advised him and three nuns and a Catholic laywoman who also lived and worked at the parish to go to Cuba to "continue your Communist work." Slogans on the door of the modest parish house that the nuns shared reflected the attitude of the ultra-right and hardliners of the military. One read, "This house lodges communists. Anyone entering will die."

Sisters Ita Ford and Maura Clarke, Maryknoll Mission Sisters, Sister Dorothy Kazel, an Ursuline, and Miss Jean Donovan, a lay missionary from Cleveland, Ohio, lived with and as the people. Their work in El Salvador, as in other parts of Central America, was to build Christian community. Although they lived a poor and meager existence, they loved the people, and in return they were loved by the people. The missionaries assisted parents preparing their children to receive the sacraments. They assisted those who were out of work to find jobs, and they labored in the fields along with the workers. They counseled with the people about God's love and plans for them.

Sisters Ford and Clarke went to Nicaragua to attend a meeting of Maryknoll sisters in Central America. They returned home on December 3, and were met at the airport by Sister Kazel and Miss Donovan. When they missed a meeting of sisters in San Salvador the next day, church authorities began a search for them. Their minibus was found stripped and burned between the airport and the capitol.

Villagers at Santa Rita Almendares in San Vicente diocese, about thirty miles from San Salvador, heard shots near midnight on the third. Because violence had been prevailing in the countryside, no one ventured out to see what was going on. Near dawn, an elderly man found a shallow grave and called the village priest, who in turn notified the archdiocesan authorities. They called a justice of the peace, who gave orders for the bodies to be unearthed. A medical report indicated that the four had been shot in the head with large-caliber bullets. All of the bodies were clad, but two were missing undergarments. The bulletin pointed out that Miss Donovan's body showed signs of sexual assault.

Security forces attempted to discourage funeral attendance. In the days before the services, however, hundreds of church workers, peasants and workers filed past the remains of the four martyrs as they lay in state at the San Jose Shrine on the grounds of the major seminary in downtown San Salvador.

An atmosphere of fear surrounded the funeral for the missioners. Military personnel were stationed in trucks parked near the church of La Libertad, and armed soldiers patrolled the square in front. Army patrols stood at access points to discourage peasants from attending the services. In his homily, Bishop Arturo Rivera Damas of Santiago de Maria, apostolic administrator of San Salvador, said, "We are oppressed but not defeated."

Between 1976 and 1980, rightist squads claimed the lives of priests, missionaries, and lay leaders of Christian communities. They murdered them because of their pastoral and social action among the poor, peasants and city workers alike. Close to 15,000 persons have died as a result of political violence, including three priests and Archbishop Oscar Romero of San Salvador. Additionally, over three hundred people are missing after being arrested or abducted.

The remains of Sister Kazel and Miss Donovan were flown to Cleveland for services and burial in the United States. Sisters Ford and Clarke, in keeping with a Maryknoll tradition and the wishes of their relatives, were buried in the village of Chalatenango. They stayed with the people they loved, for the love of God.

Sisters Maura Clarke and Ita Ford, Maryknoll Mission Sisters, Sister Dorothy Kazel, an Ursuline, and Miss Jean Donovan, lay missionary from Cleveland, Ohio. Photo courtesy of the Maryknoll Missioners.

ESTONIA
LATVIA
LITHUANIA
GERMAN DEMOCRATIC REPUBLIC
POLAND
CZECHOSLOVAKIA
HUNGARY
ROMANIA
YUGOSLAVIA
BULGARIA

Estonia

As in all parts of the Soviet Union, the constitutional guarantee of freedom of religious thought has been merely a farce in Estonia. The Communist Party has espoused atheism and barely tolerated organized religion. Many Lutheran pastors, in particular, appear to have been targeted by the government for repression, and a number of them have lost their license to practice.

All expressions of Estonian religious sentiment have been repressed by the Soviet authorities, and a number of human rights violations were reported in 1986. Cruel and inhuman treatment of political prisoners has occurred during interrogations, and during confinement in labor camps, prisons and psychiatric hospitals. In May 1985, Pavel Vezikov was sentenced by the Estonian Supreme Court to two years in a labor camp for allegedly circulating religious manuscripts. Allan Alajaan was freed in 1985 after a two-and-one-half-year term in a psychiatric hospital, to which he had been sent after an attempt to flee the Soviet Union.

Under the Soviet policy of perestroika, there has been a lessening of the repression, and a recent movement toward independence in Estonia has been taking advantage of an apparent erosion of Soviet authority. If Estonia achieves independence from the Soviet Union, there will very likely be a new birth of religious freedom there.

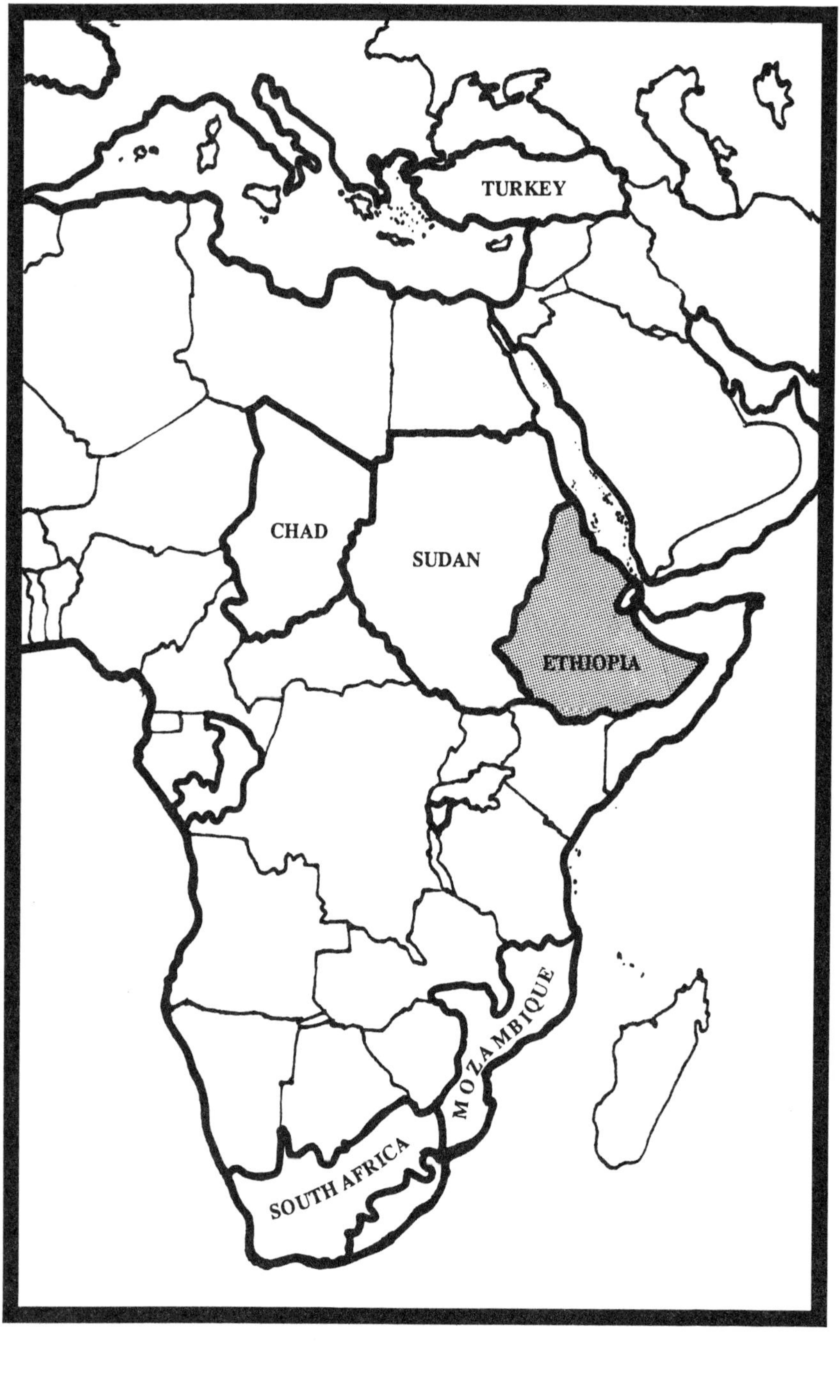
TURKEY
CHAD
SUDAN
ETHIOPIA
MOZAMBIQUE
SOUTH AFRICA

Ethiopia

There is a continuing effort to de-emphasize the importance of religion in Ethiopian life. With the overthrow of the regime of Haile Selassie, the Ethiopian Orthodox (Coptic) church lost its favored position and most of its land and property. Although the church is still allowed to function, there are government-appointed officials within the administration of the church to ensure its conformity to government policies.

Western Protestant evangelical organizations and other religions have suffered closure of churches, seizure and nationalization of property and buildings, and harassment and surveillance by government workers. In 1984, Amnesty International reported that over thirty officials of the Ethiopian Evangelical Mekane Yesus church were imprisoned for their nonviolent beliefs. A number of these were released from prison in 1986. Also in 1986 one Protestant wedding was disrupted and a number of the guests, including the groom, were jailed for illegally holding a meeting.

ESTONIA
LATVIA
LITHUANIA
GERMAN DEMOCRATIC REPUBLIC
POLAND
CZECHOSLOVAKIA
HUNGARY
ROMANIA
YUGOSLAVIA
BULGARIA

German Democratic Republic

The recent changes in the government of East Germany promise much hope for freedom of religion in that land, where until quite recently the church was openly persecuted.

Although the constitution guaranteed freedom of worship and belief, the government of East Germany officially promoted atheism. Religious activity was tolerated, although discouraged, and discrimination with regard to career advancement was common.

Some travel of religious figures was permitted, but it was strictly controlled. Secret police carefully monitored all church-sponsored events.

Although there was government pressure on the churches, the largest denomination, the Lutheran Evangelical church, remained the only institutional forum where divergent opinions could be expressed. New churches in limited numbers received government approval, although some minority sects were banned, notably Christian Scientists and Jehovah's Witnesses. Nontraditional or charismatic sects were also disallowed. Traditional religions were allowed to establish places of worship.

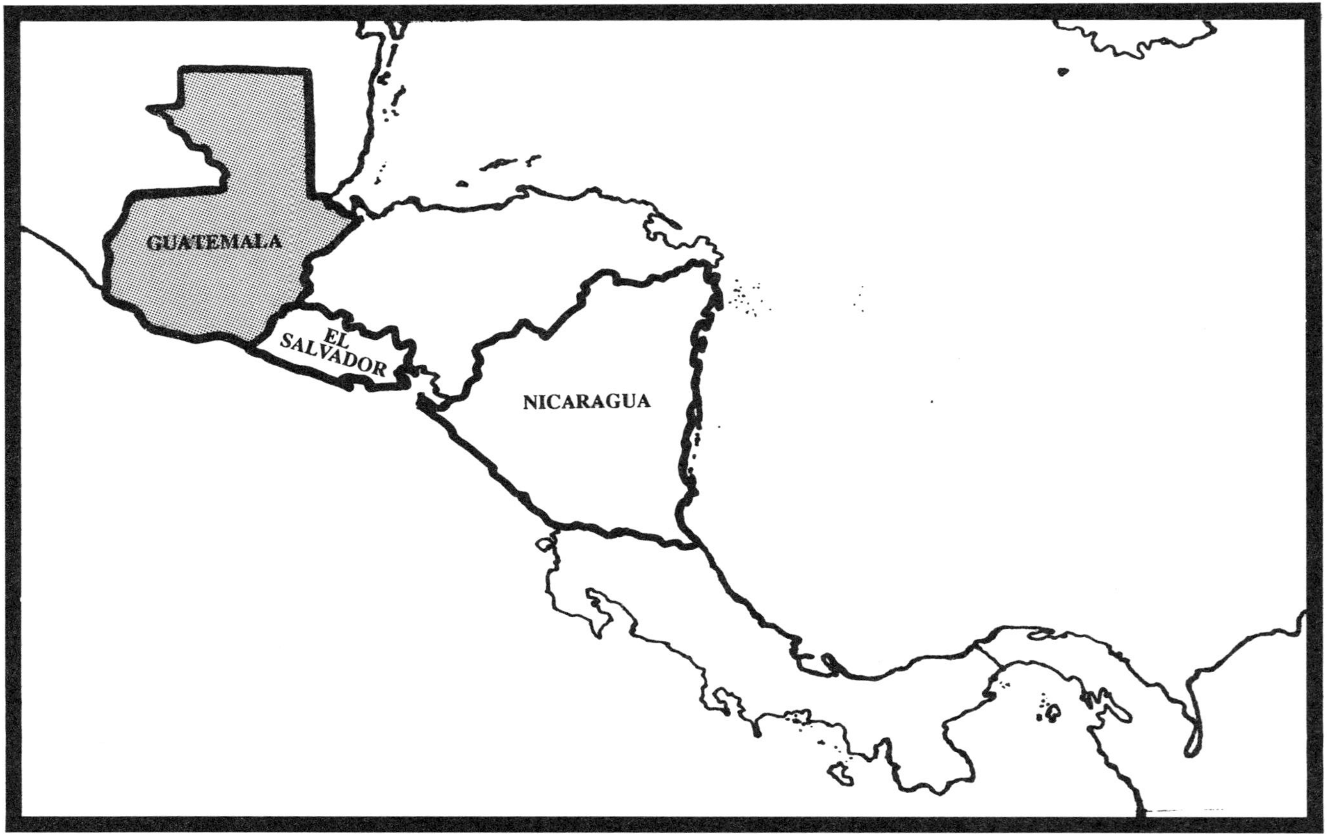
GUATEMALA
EL SALVADOR
NICARAGUA

Guatemala

Although all churches are free to preach and practice religion in Guatemala, both Catholics and Protestants have suffered from the political violence. In the late 1970's and the early 1980's, fourteen members of the Catholic clergy and hundreds of catechists lost their lives. Although several priests received death threats in 1986, no actual incidents involving violence to the Catholic clergy were reported. Four evangelical clergymen, however, were killed.

The Catholic church in Guatemala for the first time found itself working alongside a government that shared many of its concerns when the Christian Democrats came to power. It did, however, reserve its right to criticize government policies, and it has done this on a number of occasions. In particular, the archbishop has called for a more even distribution of the land.

GUYANA

BOLIVIA

C
H
I
L
E

Guyana

Although there is a constitutional guarantee of complete freedom of religion in Guyana, several incidents were reported in 1986 of harassment of churches and clergy. A British Jesuit priest was expelled in an apparent crackdown on foreign clergy who criticize government policies. Mother Teresa's Missionaries of Charity were also ordered to leave the country, although this decision was subsequently reversed. Other foreign Catholic priests who attempted to renew their residency visas were only able to obtain limited extensions. After the 1985 elections, the government-owned newspapers published personal attacks on Roman Catholic and Anglican bishops who had spoken out regarding election frauds. The homes of several church leaders who had questioned the fairness of the elections were searched.

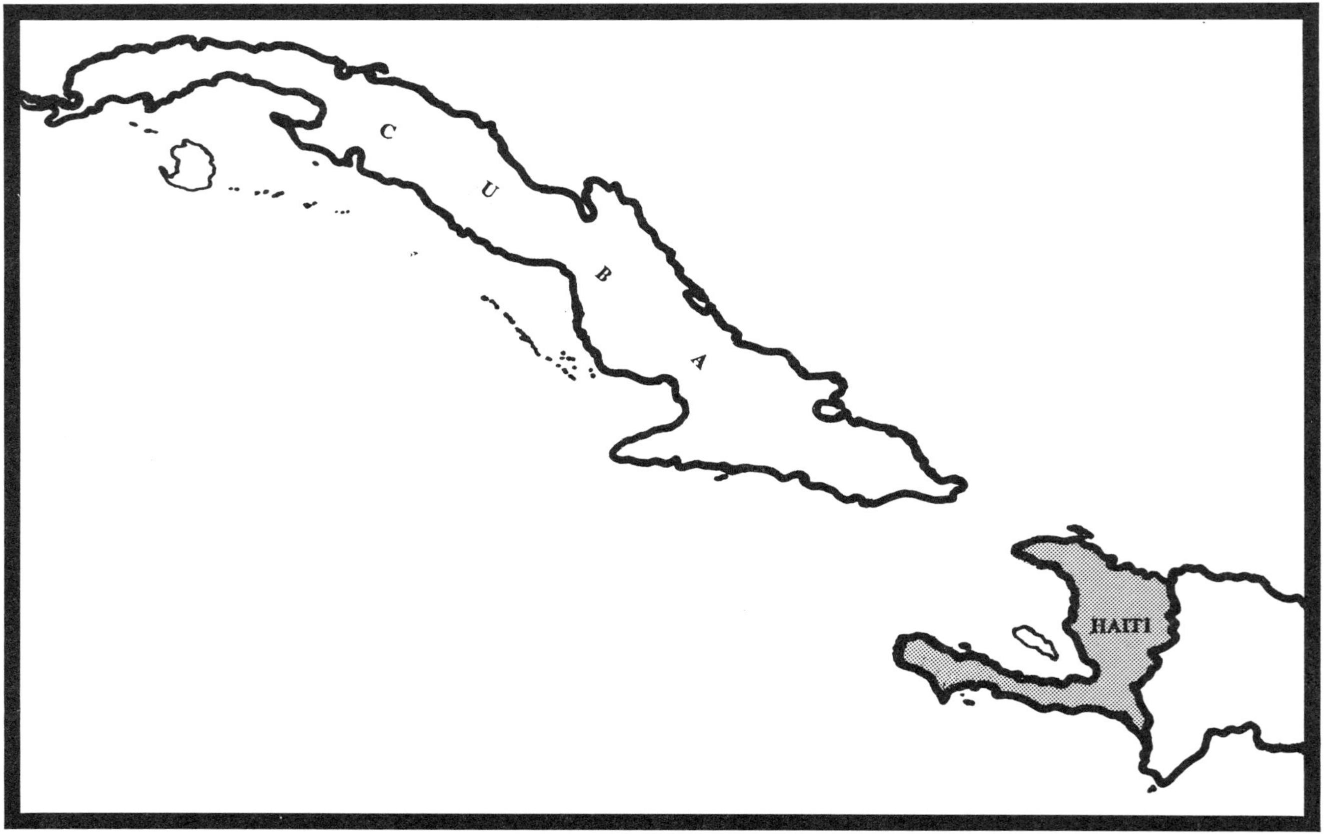
C U B A
HAITI

Haiti

Roman Catholicism is the official religion of about seventy-five percent of the population of Haiti, the poorest country in the Western hemisphere. There are no government restrictions against religion, and it usually does not interfere with missionary activity.

In September of 1986, however, Charlot Jacquelin, a Catholic church literacy worker, disappeared. Witnesses testified that several civilians and one man in military fatigues took Jacquelin from his home to a police station, where they were met by eight men in blue police uniforms who took Jacquelin away. Both civil and military officials denied any knowledge of his whereabouts.

In the last months of the Duvalier regime, the church was the island's major channel of dissent. In the summer of 1985, Radio Soleil, a popular Catholic station, denounced a sham referendum that 'reaffirmed' Duvalier as president-for-life by an unbelievable percentage of the vote. Because of this, the station's transmission lines were cut and its director, Father Hugo Triest, was arrested and expelled from the country. Two other Belgian priests were expelled and seventy-eight-year-old Father Albert DeSmet was beaten to death.

Although the new government headed by General Namphy promised reforms, there have been few improvements in the life of the average citizen of Haiti. But the Christian churches are ready to help the government act to alleviate the suffering of the people. In November 1987, in a matter of hours, a dream in Haiti dissolved in blood. The promised election, an election that to most Haitians was a vote for democracy and freedom, became a farce, and a blood bath.

The following year, 1988, saw the inauguration of a new president, Leslie Manigat. A voodoo priest was invited to preside at the inauguration ceremony—a reflection of Manigat's attitude toward Christianity.

That same year saw the murder of eleven worshipers during a Sunday Mass in Cite Soleil.

* * *

It was a lovely party. In a beautiful home in Friendswood, Texas, on January 29, 1988, about twenty-five friends of Mike and Debbie Hickey gathered to visit informally with Rev. Alain Racourt and his wife, Marlene, to talk about the church in Haiti. The Racourts were in town briefly, and Alain would be speaking the next morning to the congregation of the United Methodist Church of Friendswood.

That day, I had spoken with Rev. Don Willis in the Global Ministries division of the Methodist church in Houston. I'd asked him for information about Methodists who had suffered for their faith. He told me about Rev. Racourt's visit and suggested I contact the Friendswood church about the times he would be speaking.

The secretary at the church pleasantly instructed me to check with Debbie Hickey, as the Hickeys were making the arrangements. Mrs. Hickey graciously invited me to the get-together at her home that evening.

As usual, I was running late and the party was in full swing when I arrived. A table literally groaned with a display of taste temptations of all sorts, and with true Texas hospitality I was encouraged to fix myself a plate, help myself to coffee or soft drinks, and mix right in. Conversations were varied and animated—friends enjoying a relaxing evening with friends.

My hostess introduced me to the guests of honor. Rev. Racourt is a small man with a ready smile, a quick sense of humor, and a vivacious personality. He is soft spoken, gentle and obviously intelligent.

Marlene Racourt is a beautiful woman. My impression was that she would be a perfect subject for an artist who was trying to sculpt or paint a modern madonna, with an ephemeral smile and eyes that hint the sadness of how so many in the world daily dishonor Christ. Her silence was quickly explained: she does not speak English, but does speak French, Creole, and some Spanish. In my halting Spanish, I tried to include her in our conversation.

We chatted for a few moments, making small talk. I was happy to learn that the Racourts knew my childhood friend Gene Decker, a university professor and a Methodist lay person who has worked in Haiti. Naturally, being a mother myself, I asked about their children. With sad smiles that were explained later, they told me their children were fine and safe. Other guests joined in, and I drifted off to the kitchen to help myself to a glass of water and visit briefly.

Then the host called the guests to the living room and asked Rev. Racourt to speak. I only knew that the Racourts were guests from Haiti, and that my Methodist friends had suggested them as good information sources about the persecuted church in that country. Though I try to keep up with the news, nothing had prepared me for what Alain was speaking about in such a soft and gentle manner; his words explained the sadness in Marlene's madonna eyes.

"We are pressed on every side by troubles, but not crushed and broken," he said, quoting St. Paul. "We are perplexed because we don't know why things happen as they do, but we don't give up and quit. We are hunted down, but God never abandons us. We get knocked down, but we get up again and keep going. These bodies of ours are constantly facing death just as Jesus did; so it is clear to all that it is only the living Christ within who keeps us safe. Yes, we live under constant danger to our lives because we serve the Lord, but this gives us constant opportunities to show forth the power of Jesus Christ within our dying bodies. Because of our preaching we face death, but it has resulted in eternal life for you."

Alain told us that it is impossible for people in this country to know what it means to be free, and to enjoy the virtues of our country, such as law, order, justice, and friendship. On November 29, 1987, he and Marlene had gone into hiding for three weeks until they were able to escape from Haiti in the middle of December.

He spoke of how the Methodist church, along with other Christians in Haiti, had been working for justice, freedom, and the dignity of people. For months, church workers had explained the electoral process to three million of the people, most of whom are illiterate. They had done their work well, and by November 28, the day before the election, there were 2,277,608 people registered to vote.

Softly, Alain said, "This was their first time to vote. Do you realize you are free to elect your leaders?" After the new constitution was passed in March of 1987, Alain was chosen to be the Protestant representative on the electoral commission. There were also a Catholic representative, and seven others. The commission's job was to organize and make certain that the elections were free. He said, "I accepted when chosen, but I didn't know how risky it would be."

A few weeks before the election, Alain's family began receiving threatening phone calls at late hours. Then, on the night before the election, as Alain put it, "The world started to dissolve."

Alain reported a night of terror for his family. He spoke of hand grenades and bullets raining in his yard. One bullet went through a window and through a candle by his daughter's bed. Miraculously, none of the family was hurt. The phone was cut off, but the Racourts were able to use a portable phone to call for help. A jeep came and the Racourts were spirited away into hiding.

Hiding was, for Alain and Marlene, constant tension—a "hellish nightmare." Friends and relatives put their lives in jeopardy to protect them. At least once, there was a quick move—in fifteen minutes the "leopards" (army) would have arrived at the house where they had been.

Even at this time of fright and tension, Alain reported that there was always the feeling of being surrounded by love, affection, and care. "God works in mysterious ways," he said. The news that people in Texas, Florida, Canada, Illinois, and other places were praying for them gave them an inner power.

At last, Alain was spirited out of the country. Marlene left two days later. There was a joyous reunion in New York in December, a reunion that included their six-and-a-half-year-old granddaughter.

"Why people not like Grandad?" she asked.

As Alain told it, he had no personal enemies. He was hated because he was a representative of the church, a church working for dignity and respect for each of God's children in Haiti.

Alain told the group, "Thank you for the hope you have given us—hope, courage, and determination—as free children of God."

A question-and-answer period followed. Alain mentioned that the church in Haiti is counseled now to maintain a low profile in order to continue its work. Friends and relatives remain to continue the work in Haiti, and prayers are needed for them and for their safety. There is no question, however, that God's work should stop. He and his wife were in America on a visa that would expire in June, but were working with an attorney in an attempt to get political asylum. Finally he pointed out that the church's role in Haiti is now more important than ever. He mentioned that the church is the only institution respected in Haiti. In his words, "The church is preparing Christian citizens of tomorrow—that is where the battle will be won."

It was a lovely party. I, for one, came away with tears in my heart and a better understanding of the love and the strength of God, who stays with his apostles to the end.

GERMAN DEMOCRATIC REPUBLIC
POLAND
CZECHOSLOVAKIA
HUNGARY
ROMANIA
YUGOSLAVIA
BULGARIA

Hungary

Recent events in Hungary indicate that with the political changes will come restoration of freedom of worship, a major improvement over the situation that prevailed through autumn of 1989. In Hungary, although the state was officially committed to atheism, it opposed but did not strongly hamper religious practices. Any denomination that would accept the socialist state could be officially recognized. There were constitutional guarantees of freedom, but these were subject to restrictions. As in all parts of the Soviet bloc, a citizen's advancement could be limited by his religious beliefs. Party members were not allowed to attend religious services as believers. Party policy was to discredit religion as non-intellectual, emotional, and passe; to view religion as a relic from an earlier time.

Approximately 8.5 million of the country's close to ll million persons profess some religious belief. The largest religious groups are Roman Catholics, Reformed Calvinists, Evangelical Lutherans and Jews. Religious materials, Bibles, and newspapers are allowed, although they have been somewhat controlled by the state.

The major religions have theological training facilities and the state has permitted a limited number of new churches to be built. The Baptists, in particular, have actively been building new churches in recent years, and one new Catholic church was built near Budapest. Parents were allowed to give religious instruction to their children in their own homes.

In 1984, the Catholic church was allowed to establish a new religious order of nuns dedicated to the care of the elderly and the infirm. Additionally, the state granted the church land for a new building in Budapest to honor the golden jubilee of Cardinal Lekai.

The harassment of the church in recent years was more discreet than it once had been. The long-range goal of the government remained to create a totally secular and socialist society with no place in it for organized religion. On the other hand, the goal of the Hungarian church has been to survive and grow.

One bright spot has been in the Hungarian Catholic church. There is a movement of "base communities" who come together in groups of about a dozen at a time to pray and deepen their faith. Both Pope Paul VI and John Paul II have noted the existence of these communities with joy, calling them "the hope of the church." According to Jesuit Father Imre Andras, a Jesuit who has followed Hungarian church affairs from an institute in Vienna, there are today in Hungary from 4,000 to 6,000 such small groups.

* * *

On October 7, 1945, Bishop Jozsef Mindszenty was named Primate of Hungary. "I want to be a good shepherd who, if need be, gives his life for his flock, his Church, and his country," he said. For the next thirty-five years, the valiant shepherd stood as an example to the world of the strong faith of the Hungarian people.

In the thirty-nine months of his active primacy, he issued twenty-three pastoral letters. One of his most famous attacked the evacuation of Hungarians from southern Czechoslovakia and of long-settled Germans from Hungary. Whatever happened in politics, the cardinal remained first a pastor and a shepherd to his flock. He organized the relief of hunger in his country and went to Rome to beg for help from Pope Pius. He visited the thousands cruelly herded into camps under communist reprisals. In June of

1948 when the schools were nationalized, he ordered that all the church bells of Hungary should ring in protest. With zeal he visited the faithful, and he lived austerely, sharing his people's privations. On December 16, 1948, he called on his bishops to sign no agreements. "In an atheistic state, a Church that does not keep its independence can only play the role of a slave."

On December 23, 1947, police occupied the cardinal's house. His arrest followed three days later. He was taken to 60 Andrassy Street in Budapest, where in a cold ground-floor room he was stripped naked and given an oriental clown's outfit to wear. He was led upstairs to a cell with no bed, and he was not allowed to sleep. After his first four-hour interrogation he was returned to his cell, stripped, and beaten on every part of his body with a rubber truncheon. The cardinal finally fainted. When he came to, they demanded a confession, which he refused to sign. The beatings of the naked cardinal in front of jeering spectators continued, but still he would not sign. For thirty-nine days and nights, the torture and questioning continued. At last, Cardinal Mindszenty broke. When he signed his alleged confession, however, he wrote 'cf' by his signature—"coactus feci," meaning "signed under coercion." On February 3, 1948, the cardinal was led into court. He was sentenced to penal servitude for life.

The pope defended the cardinal before the world. "The persecution of our beloved son . . . carried out with unblushing impiety, and his brutal removal from his episcopal see, has filled us with deep sorrow."

After the trial, the communists kept Cardinal Mindszenty for a while in the hospital of the common prison. Later he was sent to a stricter prison for four years. In prison he filled his days with prayer. He prayed for the church, Hungary, his archdiocese, his fellow prisoners and his mother; he also prayed for his enemies, his guards and his persecutors. Illness increased his sufferings. His weight dropped by almost half during 1954. In May of 1954, the cardinal was moved back to the hospital of the prison in Budapest.

He was later moved to an old villa in Puspokszentlaszlo and still later to Almassy Castle near the Czechoslovakian border. At last he was offered a conditional release. "Given the choice of death in prison or freedom at the price of a shameful compromise, I prefer death," he wrote. In October of 1956, Cardinal Mindszenty was released. Bells pealed as he drove through villages, the people threw flowers, and in the capital crowds clustered at his residence, where he blessed them.

The cardinal acted at once against the peace priests, who were collaborating with the government, dissolving their movement.

Near midnight of November 3, 1956, the Soviets attacked. Thirty thousand Hungarians were soon to die. The cardinal and his secretary fled to the American embassy with their cassocks pulled up below their coats. They had to pass through the Soviet tank lines to reach the embassy. President Eisenhower granted the cardinal asylum within a half hour of his arrival.

Year after year, day and night, police sat in a car outside the embassy. They stood ready to arrest the cardinal should he leave the embassy. He could not even leave to attend the funeral of his mother in February of 1960. His life in the embassy was one of labor and prayer. In spite of a number of projected release plans, the cardinal refused any amnesty unless it involved full restoration of his position as archbishop.

In September of 1971, the Vatican drafted an agreement with the regime; a papal envoy took it to the cardinal. The cardinal was to keep his titles but lose his functions, to leave Hungary quietly, to publish nothing harmful to relations between Hungary and Rome, and to be forbidden to publish any memoirs. The cardinal refused to sign although both President Nixon and the pope advised him to do so. He only later learned that assurances of his compliance had been made on his behalf.

On his release, he was taken to Rome, where he was received with real joy by Pope Paul. The pope called him a "symbol of unshakable strength rooted in faith and in selfless devotion to the Church."

Cardinal Mindszenty decided to live in Vienna, and began a series of pastoral visits to his exiled countrymen in Europe, Canada, the United States and South Africa. The Hungarian government began to protest to the Vatican at the tone of his speeches, using intimidated bishops to demand that he be silent. The cardinal was dismayed that the enforced silence of the Hungarian church might be extended to himself, even though he was now freed. He continued his pastoral tours in 1973.

At last, the agreement Rome had been forced to make to secure his release would bring him his final and heaviest cross. Sadly and reluctantly, on November 1, the pope asked him to abdicate the see of Esztergom. The cardinal declined and continued with his plans to publish his memoirs. On the twenty-fifth anniversary of his arrest, he received a letter from the pope declaring the see vacant. Pope Paul, an honorable man, was forced to honor an agreement with men who embodied dishonor. Although the Vatican announced that he had retired, the cardinal made it clear that he had been deposed. He loyally accepted the decision of the pope, but he concluded his memoirs with these words: "This is how I arrived at complete and total exile."

Full of grief but still unbroken, the cardinal resumed his pastoral journeys. He worked too hard for a man of eighty-three, and fell ill in Bogota, Colombia. An operation seemed to help, but his heart at last gave out on May 6, 1975. His remains were buried at the shrine of Mariazell in Austria, where Our Lady is venerated as the patroness of Hungary. Some day, with God's help, they will be laid to rest in the Cathedral of Esztergom.

U. S. S. R.

MONGOLIA

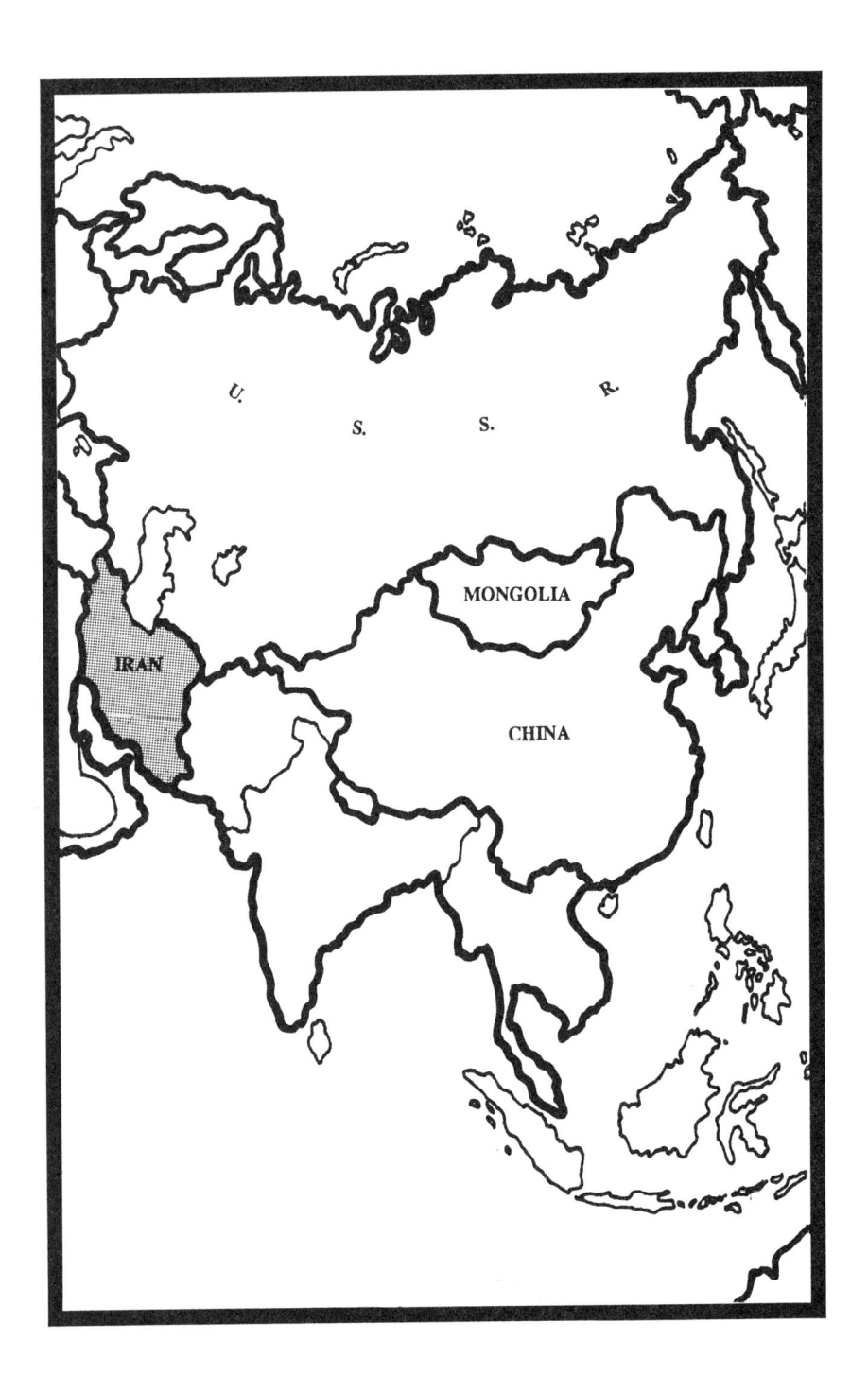

IRAN

CHINA

Iran

The small Christian population of Iran is concentrated primarily in urban areas. Minority religions are recognized in the constitution and they are permitted to practice their religions and instruct their children, and some maintain schools. There continue to be reports of severe discrimination in the areas of education, public housing and employment. The government severely discriminates against Muslims who have converted to Christianity.

Reliable statistics are not available for the number of persons jailed, tortured, or killed for political or religious reasons in recent years.

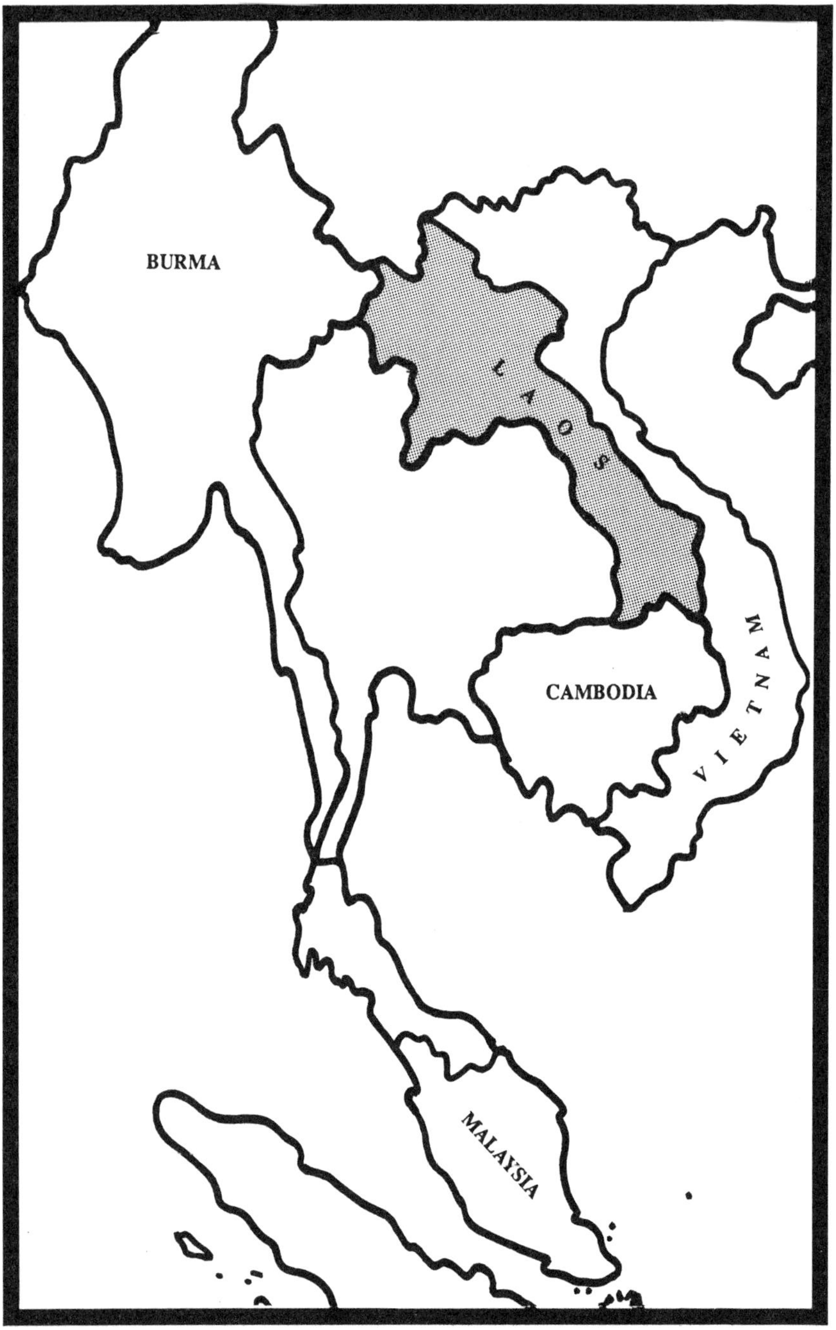
BURMA
LAOS
CAMBODIA
VIETNAM
MALAYSIA

Laos

Since 1975, the government has periodically taken over a number of Buddhist and Christian places of worship for use as public buildings. Many of the citizens believe that the government is engaged in a long-term effort to reduce the role of religion, that it considers religious activities unproductive and that it objects to a strong group of organized believers with independent beliefs.

Missionaries are not formally banned from entering the country, but in most cases no permission is given. Christians are permitted to worship, but church activities are strictly monitored. Some church leaders remain under detention, either without being charged or for alleged antiregime activity. Former prisoners in "re-education" camps have reported that punishment for misbehavior could include brutal public beatings, shackling and sometimes deprivation of food.

Christian schools, seminaries, and associations have been banned since the mid-seventies. In 1984, a new Roman Catholic bishop coadjutor of Vientiane was consecrated, and several Protestants were released from "re-education camps." Additionally, some church officials were allowed to visit the local Catholic church leaders in 1984. The Bishops of Laos, however, did not go to meet the pope during his visit to nearby Bangkok. One Catholic priest was ordained in 1986, and some short-term Protestant training sessions for clergy were permitted. In August of 1986, fifty

Catholic children were confirmed, and some foreign Catholic church officials were allowed to visit coreligionists in the country.

ESTONIA
LATVIA
LITHUANIA
GERMAN DEMOCRATIC REPUBLIC
POLAND
HUNGARY
YUGOSLAVIA
BULGARIA

Latvia

Until very recently, religious activity in Latvia suffered from continuous government harassment. Roman Catholics, Baptists, Seventh Day Adventists and Pentecostals have all encountered difficulties with the authorities. Lidija Doronina-Lasmane, a Baptist, was at last report in a prison camp in Mordovia. In spite of constitutional guarantees, religious liberty was scarce. The political changes and the move toward independence from the Soviet Union have been accompanied by the promise of renewed freedom of religion.

ESTONIA
LATVIA
LITHUANIA
POLAND
CZECHOSLOVAKIA
HUNGARY
ROMANIA
BULGARIA

Lithuania

Like its neighbor Latvia, Lithuania too has recently experienced political changes that may make the constitutional guarantees of religious freedom in Lithuania more than words. Not long ago, the Soviet authorities had apparently mounted a large-scale attack on all religious activities not directly controlled by the state. In particular, the Lithuanian Catholic church was the subject of harsh treatment.

The government took control of church committees, severely limited enrollment in the only seminary, harassed children who attempted to attend services, and forced school children to join atheistic organizations. Historic shrines and artifacts belonging to the church were desecrated or destroyed, and physical attacks on persons attending religious festivities were not uncommon.

The Lithuanian Catholic Committee for the Defense of Believers' Rights was forced underground. Three Catholic priests—Fathers Jonas Matulionas, Alfonsas Svarinkas and Sigitas Tamkevicius—were in prison, and a Catholic student, Roman Zemaitis, was serving two years in a labor camp.

Lithuanian activists have died in Soviet custody, but it is usually impossible to prove official involvement in their deaths.

In February of 1986, Father Juozas Zdebskis was killed in a mysterious car accident after having been warned several times by the authorities to cease his activities with the Catholic Committee for the Defense of Believers' Rights. In August of 1985, another of the Committee members, Father Vaclovas Stakenas, was attacked, and Lithuanian activists pointed out the similarity of the attack to the one that killed Father Popieluszko in Poland in 1984.

It appears to many as if the more harshly the sturdy Lithuanian Catholics are treated, the more active and vigorous they become. A samizdat report, the *Chronicle of the Catholic Church in Lithuania*, has routinely been smuggled out of the country and republished with a large circulation in the Free World. The *Chronicles* detail all of the ways the Soviets officially harass and persecute the church. Several small Protestant sects have also been the target of official harassment.

* * *

On February 5, 1986, Father Juozas Zdebskis was killed in an automobile collision, under suspicious circumstances. Two of three other occupants of the car also died.

On February 10, the Lithuanian State Department of Motor Vehicles reported that the car Father Zdebskis was driving crossed the center lane and collided with a milk truck. Supposedly, the cause of the collision was to be investigated. Tass, reporting the incident to the world abroad, told a slightly different version of the story. According to the Tass version, the priest's car was attempting to pass another car when it ran into the milk truck. Neither report mentioned the truck driver's name. If there was another vehicle, no report of its occupants was made. Many of the Lithuanian Catholics in the area believe that this collision was not accidental, but a carefully planned and executed act of violence, one more in the chain of persecutions of the Roman Catholic believers of Lithuania.

The day of his death, the telephone of the rectory at Rudamina, where Father Zdebskis was pastor, was disconnected. Friends learned of the collision a day later. The one survivor who was riding in the priest's car, Zemaitis, contradicted himself when he told his first visitors in the hospital about the accident. Later, he was forbidden to have visitors. On his release, he wrote a panegyric to the Soviet friendship of nations for a local newspaper, and expressed his gratitude for the medical treatment given to him. The funeral itself was kept under observation by KGB agents, and those helping were followed for several days. There were about one hundred priests participating in the solemn ceremonies, and countless throngs of the faithful, especially young people. One frozen youth, keeping vigil in the unheated church, told a priest friend of Father Zdebskis, "He gave me God."

Father Juozas Zdebskis was born in 1929, in Mindaugai. In 1948, after completing his intermediate education, he entered the seminary in Kaunas. He was ordained a priest in 1952. Father Zdebskis's first parish was Siluva. Later, he worked in other parishes, and pursued higher studies in theology. While serving as pastor at Gudeliai, he was sentenced to a year in prison for catechizing children. Prison did not break the priest's spirit, but rather strengthened it. Together with Father Sigitas Tamkevicius, he wrote a petition for more seminarians to be allowed to enter the Kaunas Seminary. For their boldness in writing the petition, the two priests lost their registration certificates and the right to function officially as priests. For a year, the two were obliged to work as laborers in land reclamation. In the time he was free from physical labor, Father Zdebskis continued in his apostolate. Thereafter, the Soviet authorities allowed him to return to work as a parish priest.

In Prienai, Father Zdebskis was one of the first to assemble children and youths, allowing them to serve at Mass. He directed youth retreats and was a zealous helper to the Friends of the Eucharist. At last, he was arrested a second time for catechizing children and sentenced to a year in camp.

After returning from prison, he was named pastor of Slavantai. The authorities thought that his work in such an out-of-the-way parish would be restricted. However, Father Zdebskis involved many priests and laity in the active struggle for the revival of the

Catholic faith in Lithuania, and for the defense of basic human rights.

Up to 1972, there had been no organized voice for persecuted Lithuanian 1982, the first issue of the underground *Chronicle of the Catholic Church in Lithuania* appeared and began to document human rights violations around the country on a systematic basis.

In 1978, five Catholic priests took a further step, and founded a Catholic Committee for the Defense of Believers' Rights. Father Zdebskis was an active participant in the creation of this group. The goal of this committee was to obtain for believers rights equal to those of atheists. The priests began issuing public appeals on specific cases of religious persecution. Through the years, the ranks of the committee increased, including the addition of one lay member who is now in labor camp. Two of the committee's charter members, Fathers Alfonsas Svarinskas and Sigitas Tamkevicius were imprisoned in 1983. Following their arrests, the remaining members came under severe government attack. They were summoned for questioning, searched, threatened with arrest and asked to resign. Eventually, the committee was forced underground.

In 1988 Father Svarinskas was released. His health had been ruined, however, by the twenty-plus years he had spent in Soviet labor camps and prisons.

Father Zdebskis seemed tireless. If he was not able to complete his sick calls during the day, he would go at night. If the road was poor, he would go on foot. He often traveled hundreds of kilometers to visit with and take the sacraments to soldiers or to sick and elderly Catholics. He often traveled to the exiles in the depths of Russia. He went to the faithful of Tadzhik, Armenia, the Volga Basin and others who had been left with churches but without priests. He often attended the trials of prisoners of conscience.

After trials, warnings and threats, the Soviet government took terrorist measures against the priest. Under suspicious circumstances he was burned, with some parts of his body suffering third-degree burns. Allegedly because he had been driving after drinking (he was a strict abstainer), his driver's license was revoked. On several occasions, accidents were set up, and a series of raids and interrogations occurred.

Father Zdebskis was assigned as pastor of Rudamina, where he worked until his tragic death. A written eulogy by the Friends of the Eucharist reads in part: "Nowadays, we proudly proclaim that the first Lithuanian book was the catechism; [Father Zdebskis] defended our right to open the catechism, paying for it with his freedom in labor camp. He showed us a God who is near, dwelling in our midst. He gave us Jesus, present in our love for one another. When everything was frozen in the grip of overbearing brutality, terror and fear; when all of us waited like rabbits to scatter at the first sound, he would secretly gather us into small groups, he would organize meetings, open the Friends of the Eucharist rule-book, and we would hear 'With God on our side who can be against us?'"

Had he lived a while longer, he would have celebrated his thirty-fifth anniversary of ordination. The quotation on his tombstone expresses well the hallmark of his life. It reads, "Love does not come to an end" (1 Cor. 13:8).

The founding members of the Catholic Committee for the Defense of Believers' Rights: Fr. Sigitas Tamkevicius, Fr. Vincas Velavicius, Fr. Juozas Zdebskis, Fr. Alfonsas Svarinskas and Fr. Jonas Kauneckas. Photo courtesy of Lithuanian Information Center.

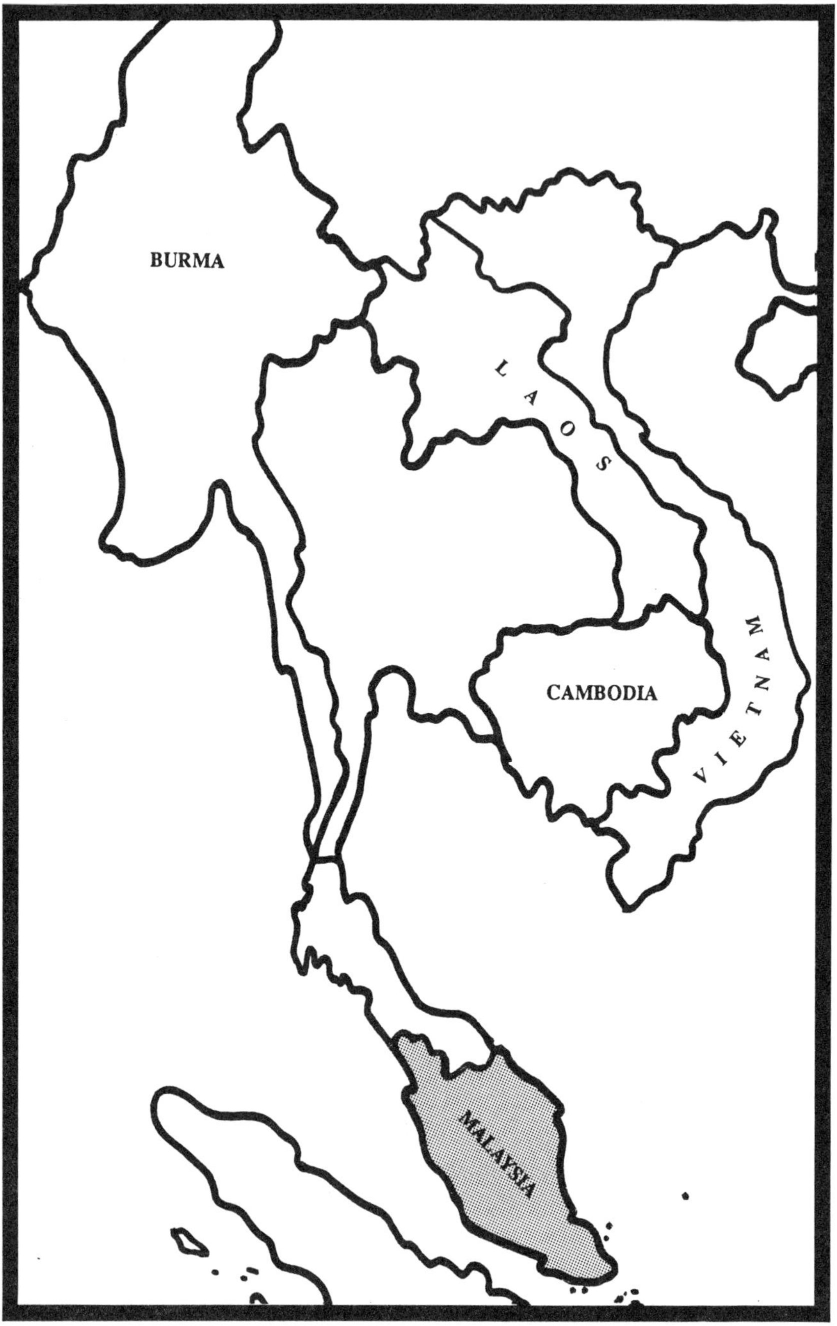

BURMA
LAOS
VIETNAM
CAMBODIA
MALAYSIA

Malaysia

Inside Malaysia's Persecuted Church

by Rev. Paul Marx, President, Human Life International

This nation of 127,316 square miles, slightly larger than New Mexico, is home to 17 million people of many races and religions. Geographically, it comprises the Malay Peninsula and the states of Sarawak and Sabah on the island of Borneo; 600 miles of ocean separate Borneo and the peninsula. This well-developed, enormously well-endowed country is free of all weather hazards. But the climate is always hot, wet and humid.

In 1511 the Portuguese established a trading post known today as the city of Malacca. With them came some Jesuits, including St. Francis Xavier, who later made Malacca his stopping-off place for his oriental mission journeys. Later the Dutch arrived; the English took over in 1867.

The Paris Foreign Mission Society and the English Mill Hill Fathers were the real pioneer missionaries, coming in large numbers. In 1852 the Christian Brothers arrived, eventually establishing some sixty-three schools, with more than one hundred brothers teaching. At one time there were more than 130 Catholic mission schools in Malaysia. When the British were in charge, they sent their children to the Catholic schools, which provided educated workers.

The Moslems had arrived centuries before the rest, coming as Arab traders. After Malaya separated from England in 1957, Malaysia was formed in 1963.

Malaysia is 55% Malay Moslems, 35% Chinese (Buddhist or Taoist), 8% Hindu Indians and the remaining 2% mostly Catholic, from a variety of ethnic backgrounds, including some Eurasians. Malay is the official language, but one-third of the people speak English.

There are 4,000 Catholic Malaysians for every priest. The priest shortage is great: in my 1990 visit to the country, I met two priests who cared for 102 mission stations, traveling among them to care for thousands of parishioners. In the early seventies, the increasingly militant Moslem government expelled all foreign priests and religious. For example, the diocese of Kota Kinabalu at one time had sixty-seven priests, but in 1990 had only twenty-nine. Missionaries may come in only selectively, and may stay no more than ten years.

Three priests take care of all 17,000 parishioners at the cathedral parish of Kuching, plus several outlying mission stations with 10,000 more souls! Malaysia has fewer than 200 priests and only about 350 religious. Fortunately, only one order of nuns has cast off the habit (and they have few vocations). As in Africa, the Church employs professional catechists to teach the faith to young people.

I spoke with five of Malaysia's seven bishops, and at length with Archbishop Anthony Soter Fernandez of Luala Lampur, the capital. The bishops impressed me—they have a very difficult task because of the Moslems' persecution, which is both subtle and satanic. Nowhere have I found the Moslems more militantly anti-Catholic—a harbinger of the future elsewhere! Already there are more Moslems than Catholics in the world, and Islam is the fastest-growing religion.

Malaysia purports to be a parliamentary democracy, with a periodically changing Moslem monarch, but in fact it's an Islamic dictatorship—and a land of many contradictions and contrasts. For example, the state of Sabah has a Catholic governor, although he's undermined and much opposed.

But to the followers of Mohammed, all non-Moslems are infidels. Only after much agonized pleading and many delays are the bishops allowed to erect buildings. To advance professionally you must become a Moslem. Christians are bribed to become Moslems with job offers, promotions and money. Moslems are forbidden to become Christians.

The government has virtually taken over all Catholic hospitals and schools. Moslem authorities appoint school principals and faculty, and even decide which children go to what school. Only Islam may be officially taught in school. Christians teach their faith in Sunday school and, at times, on Saturday, and sometimes illegally during the week (on private property). The Catholic schools, as is always true of mission countries, were far superior to the others, and still are today, insofar as they exist.

The Moslems also control all three TV channels and the radio networks. The Christians have no access to them. Religious police enforce the month-long Ramadan fast. Also, if they find a boy and girl together at night, the lovers are fined, jailed or both.

Planned Parenthood has "clinics," usually attached to hospitals, all over the country. The government funds these, but they're meant primarily for the Christians, to whom they give the Pill and condoms. In the countryside Planned Parenthood inflicts on women the abortifacient Depo-Provera, an injectible potion so dangerous that it's illegal in America. Pro-life doctors estimated that one out of every five pregnancies was being illegally aborted. The prime minister has said he wants a population of 70 million (up from 17 million) by the year 2000—preferably Moslems. The depopulation program seems, therefore, to have no aim but that of reducing the Christian population. While there is some poverty in the countryside, there is surely no hunger. The landscape is lush with native fruits and vegetables; fish are always available in nearby waters. Crops are raised year round; rice is harvested three times a year and some vegetables every six weeks!

The government gets the money for these depopulation "clinics" from the United Nations Fund for Population Activities (UNFPA), the greatest promoter of contraceptives and abortifacients in the world. The International Planned Parenthood Federation (IPPF) seems to be guiding the depopulation program. Before my visit, neither the bishops nor the lay Catholic leaders seemed to know who these family-destroyers (Planned Parenthood) were or what they did. Human Life International is supporting the bishops in their education program by providing videos, films and printed materials. The saintly archbishop of Kuching, Peter Chang Hoan Ting, has a Catholic videocassette lending library.

In no country of the world have I been so welcomed by the bishops, priests and nuns! I met with many leadership and training groups, advising them on how to enhance marriage and family life, promote natural family planning (NFP), and resist Planned Parenthood. Malaysia must have the world's best-organized Catholic Nurses Guild, guided by the renowned social worker Richard Lai. This may explain why the country has over one hundred NFP teachers. In the developing countries and in their struggling Church you meet the finest Catholics and the most beautiful children.

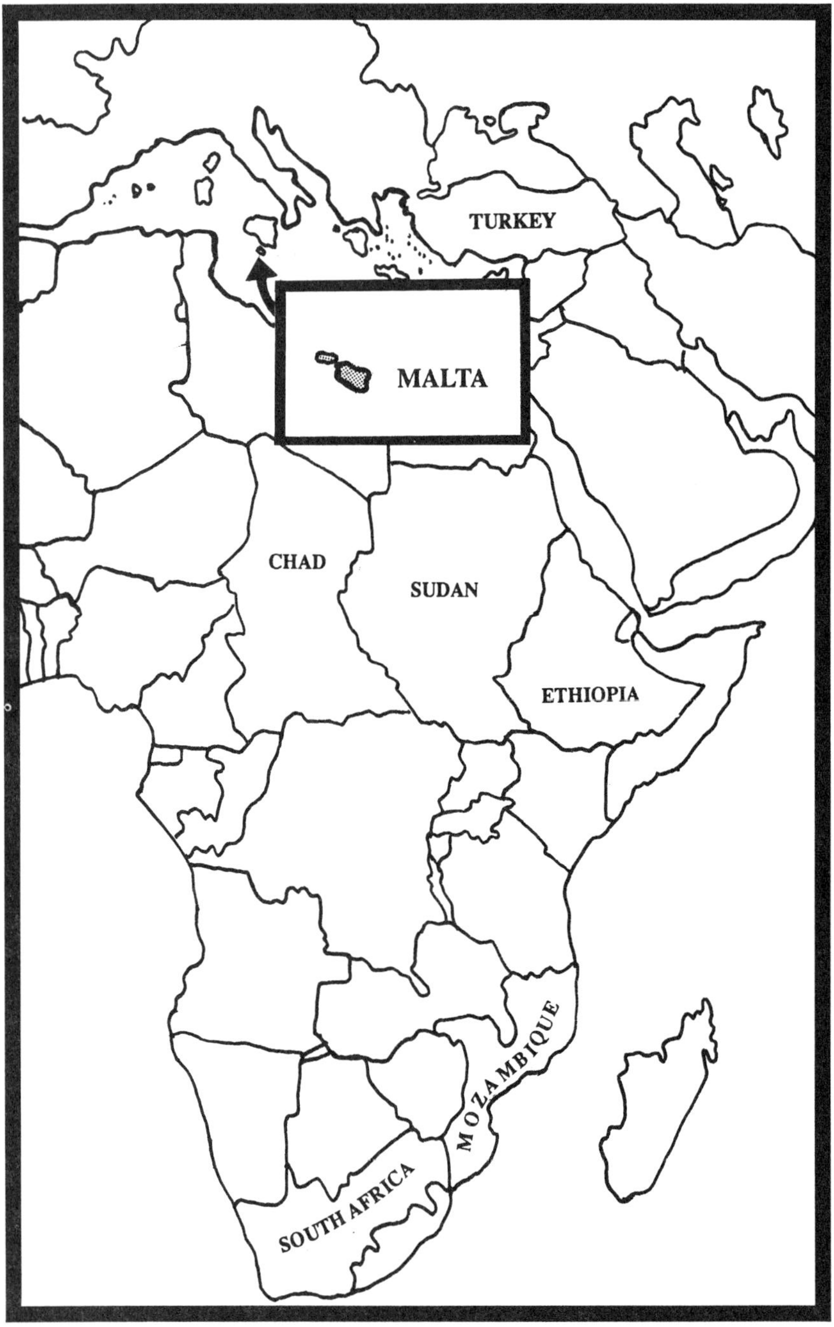
TURKEY
MALTA
CHAD
SUDAN
ETHIOPIA
MOZAMBIQUE
SOUTH AFRICA

Malta

The status of the church in Malta is shaky. Under the left-oriented regime of Dominick Mintoff, there was a strong confrontation between the church and state, especially in 1984. The main problem was the church-state conflict over Catholic schools. The government attempted to force the closing of the Catholic high schools by prohibiting them from charging tuition, and it threatened to take over church property. The Mintoff government made no secret of its aim to make education the mouthpiece for socialist doctrine. The Vatican sent a papal nuncio in February of 1986, and an interim agreement was signed in July. Two longstanding cases involving church property and schools are still not completely resolved.

Under the Mintoff administration, Catholic hospitals and charitable institutions also suffered problems. In a number of cases, buildings and property have simply been expropriated, and little if any attempt made to reimburse the Maltese Diocese or the religious orders for the loss of the property.

In May of 1987, Prime Minister Edward Fenech Adami and the conservatives were elected by a narrow margin, the first time the conservatives had been in power in sixteen years. Adami promised to guarantee full liberty to the Catholic church, and to correct the wrongs of the previous regime.

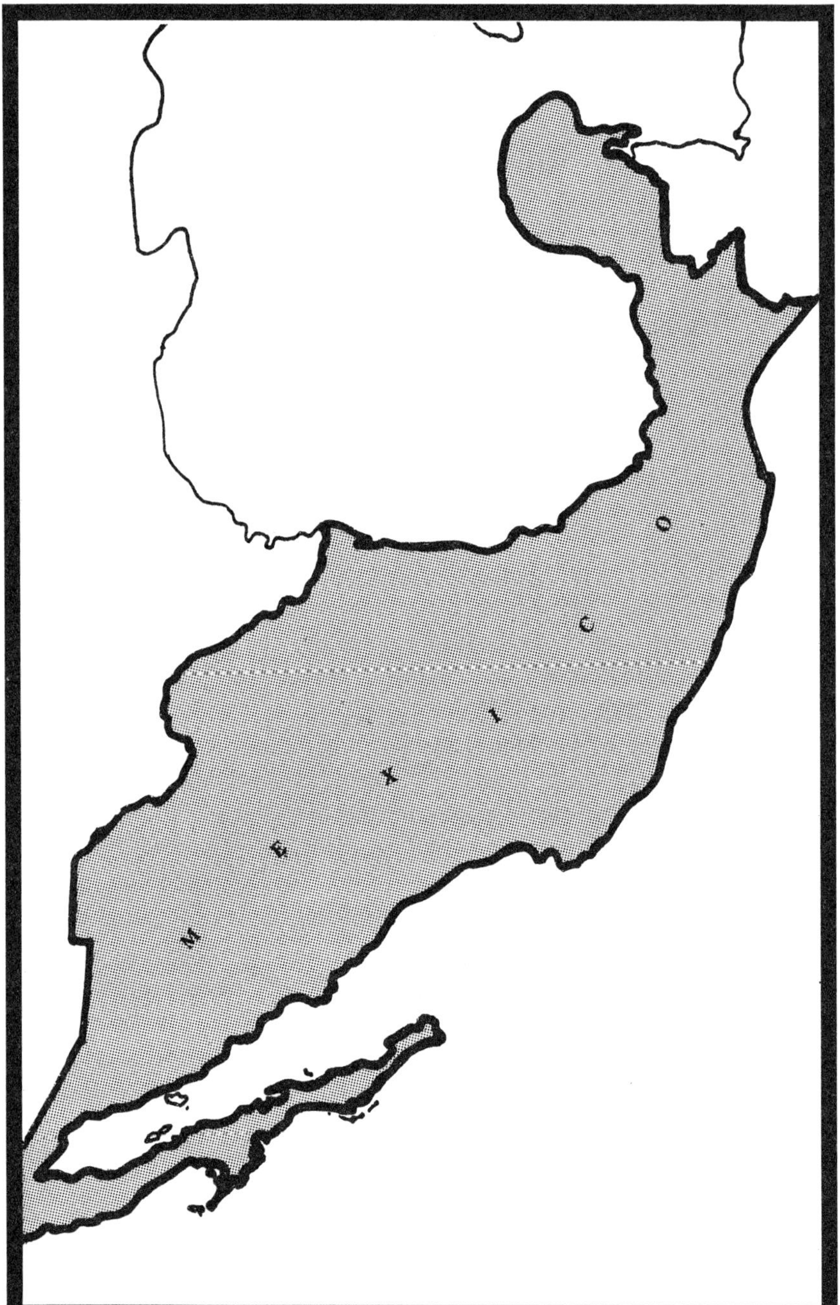
M E X I C O

Mexico

Considered worldwide to be a Catholic country, the constitution of Mexico guarantees everyone the freedom to practice the religion of choice. However, no religious body has any legal existence, and there are severe restrictions on the clergy and the church. Although in recent years many of the restrictive laws have been relaxed or ignored, the laws could in any given instance be enforced. The clergy are prohibited from active participation in politics, voting, owning real estate or wearing religious habit in public.

A new law passed in 1986 sets stiff fines for any clergy found guilty of inducing the electorate to vote for or against a political candidate.

There is a constitutional restriction against pre-university religious schools, although many of these do, in fact, exist. In religious schools the government has mandated the textbooks to be used. A number of religious educators have criticized this practice, complaining in particular of the books' treatment of the free-enterprise system.

As of early 1990, the Mexican government was considering an official restoration of liberty, including abolition of the anti-clerical laws.

In 1984, fifty-two Evangelical missionaries were expelled from Chihuahua. The government invoked article 130 of the constitution, which prohibits holding religious services outside of church buildings and homes.

In 1986 a group of basic Christian communities in northern Mexico protested social conditions in a formal document, stating that an unjust social system had caused the poor and unemployed to be the hardest-hit victims of the country's economic crisis.

In April of 1987, two Mexican leftist political parties broke with tradition and called for the right of Catholic priests, nuns and bishops to vote in elections. Although they called for extending the right to vote to the clergy, they maintained the fundamental left view that the church itself should not be allowed to own property or to be active politically.

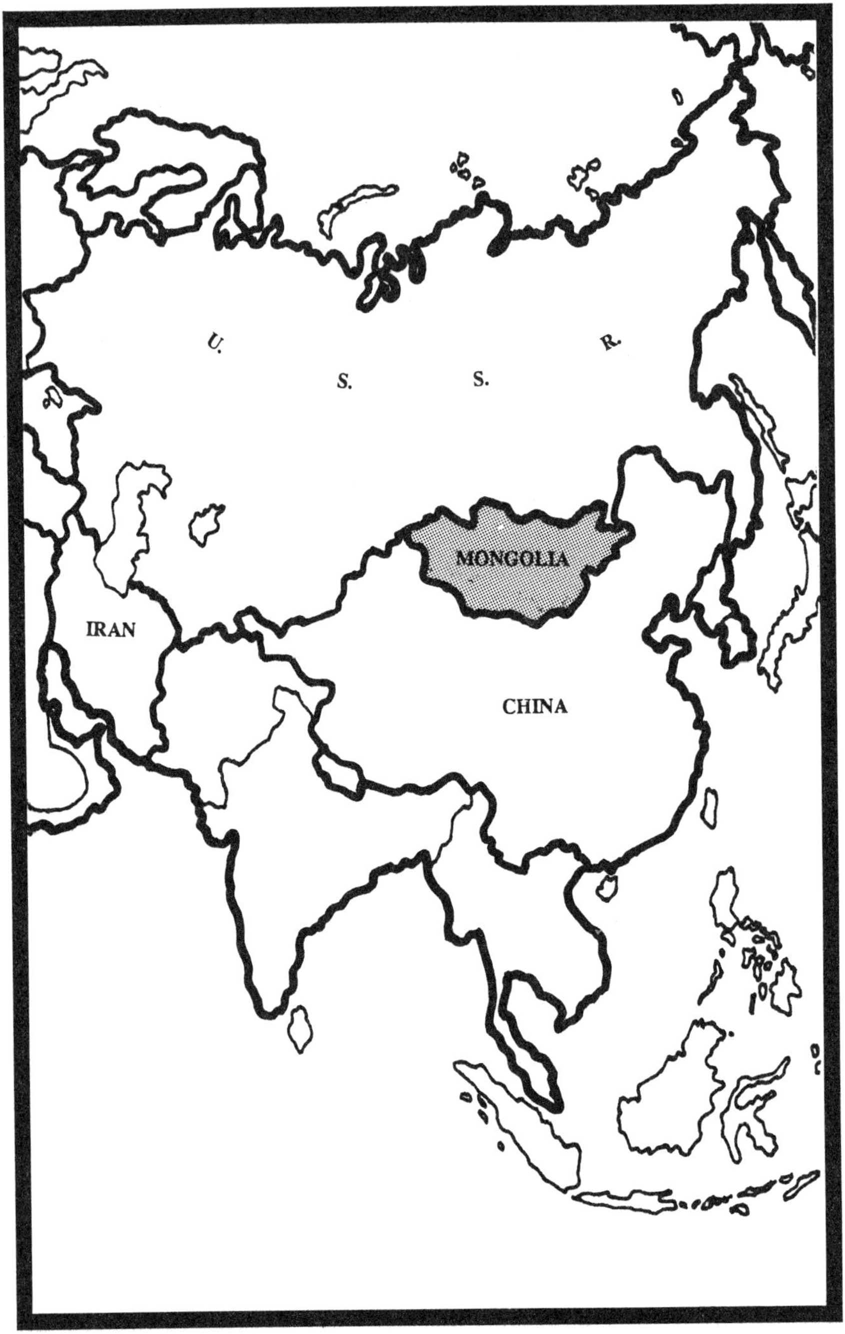
U.
S.
S.
R.
MONGOLIA
IRAN
CHINA

Mongolia

Mongolia, or the Mongolian People's Republic, is a tightly controlled communist state. There is little information available about the government treatment of Mongolian citizens.

Although religious freedom exists in theory, an Office of Religious Affairs attached to the Council of Ministers strictly controls all activity. Apparently religion has no significant part in the lives of most Mongolians. Before the establishment of the communist government, the Buddhist religion was a major force in this country. Today there are only a few monasteries with a handful of monks. These seem to be mainly for showing to the tourists, and for government propagandists. No known religious figure holds a high position in the government.

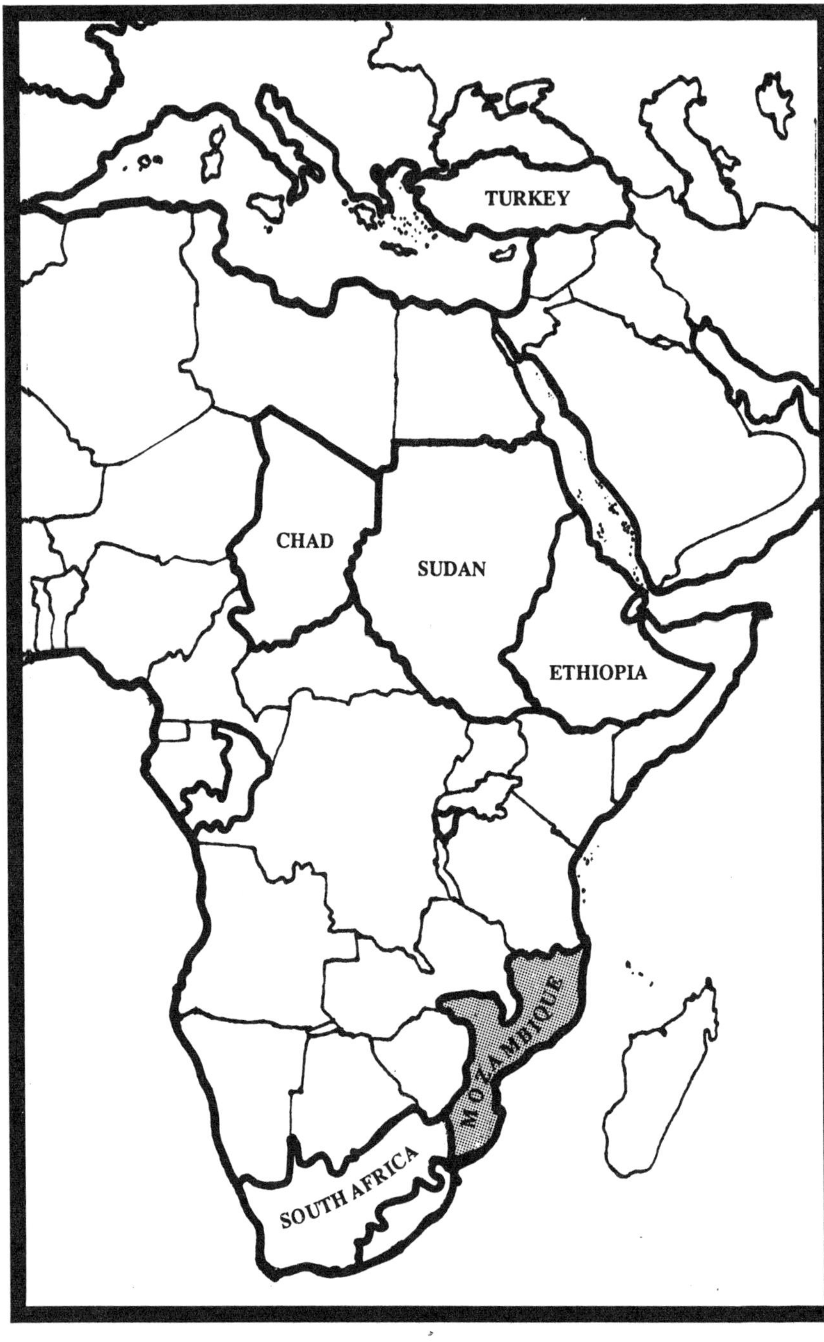
TURKEY
CHAD
SUDAN
ETHIOPIA
MOZAMBIQUE
SOUTH AFRICA

Mozambique

Since the late 1970's, there has been an increasingly violent civil insurgency in Mozambique. The country gained its independence from Portugal in 1975, following ten years of warfare by the Front for the Liberation of Mozambique (Frelimo), now the Marxist government in power in the one-party country. Since the late seventies, the Mozambican National Resistance (RENAMO) has waged an increasingly violent war against the government.

According to several reports, including those by Amnesty International, RENAMO has tortured, maimed and mistreated both military and civilian prisoners. One frequently reported technique is to cut off the noses, ears and lips of those believed to sympathize with the government; thousands of Mozambicans have undergone such disfigurement. RENAMO has charged, however, that on several occasions Frelimo forces perpetrated the killings of civilians and then blamed the incidents on RENAMO. RENAMO has reportedly abducted thousands of rural villagers, and has also kidnapped foreigners. In August of 1986, it released five Portuguese and Italian nuns, and in December another sixty-five hostages. The Council of Catholic Bishops of the country has publicly decried the killing and mutilation of prisoners both by the government and by the insurgents.

Although the constitution promises freedom of religion and separation of church and state, the government has placed a number of restrictions on the activities of religious groups. It nationalized a number of church schools and hospitals and has reserved the right to decide if individual church buildings can be used as places of worship. Church-state relations are improving slowly, and the churches are able to operate without official government harassment. In 1986, some Catholic bishops circulated a number of pastoral letters that were critical of the government, and there were no official reprisals. Two articles dealing with the Protestant church's positive role in Mozambique were published in a government magazine.

A number of the churches have been active in distributing emergency food supplies to the poorest sections of the country.

Most of the churches in the country are open and the services seem well attended. Membership in a church or mosque no longer is precluded by party membership.

Critical comments about religion by the government are mainly general in nature and not directed at a single religious target, although the practice of traditional African religions is ridiculed and criticized.

* * *

The refrain to an old hymn goes like this:

"I sing because I'm happy.
I sing because I'm free.
His eye is on the sparrow,
And I know He watches me."

One who would joyfully join in this song, and who knows full well what the author meant, is Kindra Bryan, a twenty-eight-year-old pediatric nurse at Texas Children's Hospital in Houston.

"I could tell you hundreds of stories of God's miraculous protection," Kindra said. In what she calls "more of a spiritual journey than a physical one," Kindra walked for three months and hundreds of miles through Mozambique in the summer of 1987 as a captive of the RENAMO guerilla forces.

A graduate of Texas A & M, Kindra felt drawn to missionary work in Africa. A member of Houston's Second Baptist church, Kindra wanted to go and do relief work and share Christ in the process. She said she prayed about her idea, and then wrote to a number of organizations.

A friend of Kindra's from college had been working for some time with a group called Youth With a Mission at a hospital on the Thai-Cambodian border, and suggested that Kindra apply as a volunteer with them. This interdenominational organization is active in many countries in the world, and is highly respected by many governments. Kindra applied, was accepted for work in Africa, and left in April 1987 for Harare, Zimbabwe. Here she spent about a month arranging for a visa to Mozambique, a country which has only been open to missionaries for a few years.

Kindra's original plans called for her to work in a government hospital in Beira. Four days before her scheduled departure, however, she met Roy and Trish Perkins, an Australian couple who run a farm in rural Mozambique. The Perkins ran the farm for the owner, a German baroness, and for the benefit of the people in the area. They did relief work, distributing food and clothing from Western countries. They had no medical facilities in the area, so they were in the process of building a clinic, and needed nursing staff.

Again, Kindra prayed to know God's will for her life. She knew it would be more dangerous working at the mission, but felt that the people needed her, and that she might be of more benefit there. On a Saturday, she arrived at the farm to begin setting up the health clinic. The farm was more modern than most in the country. A citrus grove and chickens helped to provide the food that is so scarce in most parts of the country. Running water and electricity are also rare. Although Kindra was aware that a war was going on in the country, it did not seem close to her.

The next Thursday, at about one in the morning, Kindra was awakened by Phil and Vicki Cooper, who, along with their twenty-month-old daughter, were staying at the farm. Kindra was told that the house was surrounded by rebels, and she and the Coopers went into an interior bathroom and locked the doors.

At first, Kindra said, she was terribly frightened, having heard stories of the torture, mutilation, and rape the rebels are known to practice on their victims. Filled with fear, she listened as the rebels broke the windows, shouted, and ransacked the farm house. Because of her great fear, at first she couldn't feel any sense of God's presence. Then she began to pray, and after twenty minutes of prayer in the dark bathroom, she began to feel as if God were speaking to her heart. He reminded her of His promises of heaven, and that He was in control. She seemed to feel that He was telling her that she had not been stupid to come to Africa, and that, as she came at His direction, He would take care of her. Kindra said that she began to feel peaceful, ready for death at such time as God should choose, and that God was in charge and would take care of everything.

At last, the soldiers broke into the bathroom and discovered Kindra and the Coopers. None of the soldiers spoke English, so by motions they gestured that the prisoners should go outside, where they were joined by the Perkins and by Joan Godwin, another nurse, who was in her late fifties. After the soldiers finished their destruction, they lined the prisoners up in front of them for a forced march, which lasted over a day. Joan had not been able to find a pair of shoes, so she and Kindra shared one pair between them.

The captives at first thought they were being lined up to be shot, but finally came to the realization that they were being taken hostage. Roy pleaded, in Portuguese, with the captors, begging them to at least allow the Coopers and the baby to stay behind, but to no avail. For the first few hours, the baby's mother carried her and attempted to feed her as she walked, for fear the baby would cry and call down the wrath of the captors. Later, Phil carried the baby for most of the way.

For months, each day was a forced march of from twelve to

fifteen hours. The captors eventually communicated that they would not harm the prisoners and would take them to a place of safety where they could be released. Their way took them through small villages, through jungles, swamps, and finally to a rain forest in the mountains where they stayed for five weeks before their eventual release.

When originally captured, Kindra had on a summer nightgown and was able to pull on a pair of warm-up bottoms. She was allowed to take a single change of clothes. She remembers vividly not being able to brush her teeth or wash her hair. The group bathed in rivers when they came to them, but often went for six or seven days between baths. When there was water, they washed their underwear at night.

In the mountains it was cold, and as Kindra put it, "We found a number of creative ways to keep warm." One way was to heat rocks in the campfire, wrap them in cloth and put them in bed. Through daily use, she began to learn the language. During this time, Kindra suffered from malaria, dysentery, and a tropical disease called bilharzia. Miraculously, some anti-malaria medicine and some aspirin were found among the items that had been taken from the farm.

Toward the end of the journey, because of sheer exhaustion, Vicki and Joan had to be carried on stretchers much of the way. The entire group was in poor physical condition. Phil was too exhausted to carry the baby farther, and the soldiers took turns carrying her. The captors seemed to treat the prisoners with kindness. At last, the group was released and allowed to leave through Malawi.

On her return home, Kindra was surprised and happy to learn of all those who had been praying for her safety—in the United States, in England, and in Africa. She received hundreds of letters, and said that she had proof of the many little things that God did to take care of them. One friend mentioned that at a prayer vigil he attended, the scripture verse about stepping on snakes and scorpions and yet being unharmed kept returning to his mind. Thinking back, Kindra realized that this prayer vigil was held on the same day that a black momba, one of the most dreaded snakes in Africa, had gotten into their camp, and that miraculously no one had been harmed.

"I'm not saying it wasn't hard, but I would do it again. I learned a lot about myself," said Kindra. "If anything, it has deepened my love for the people of Africa. A lot of missionaries go to Africa, and at least plan on taking a toothbrush and a tin of tuna. We had nothing, but God provided for everything."

Kindra resumed her nursing in the recovery room at Texas Children's hospital, and started work on her master's thesis in public health from the University of Texas. Africa is never far from her mind or her heart, however, and depending on the progress of her thesis she made plans to return to the dark continent as soon as possible.

[Readers interested in lay mission work for Youth With a Mission may write to: PACU (Pacific and Asia Christian University, 75-5851 Kuakini Highway, Kalius-Kona, Hawaii 96740-2199.]

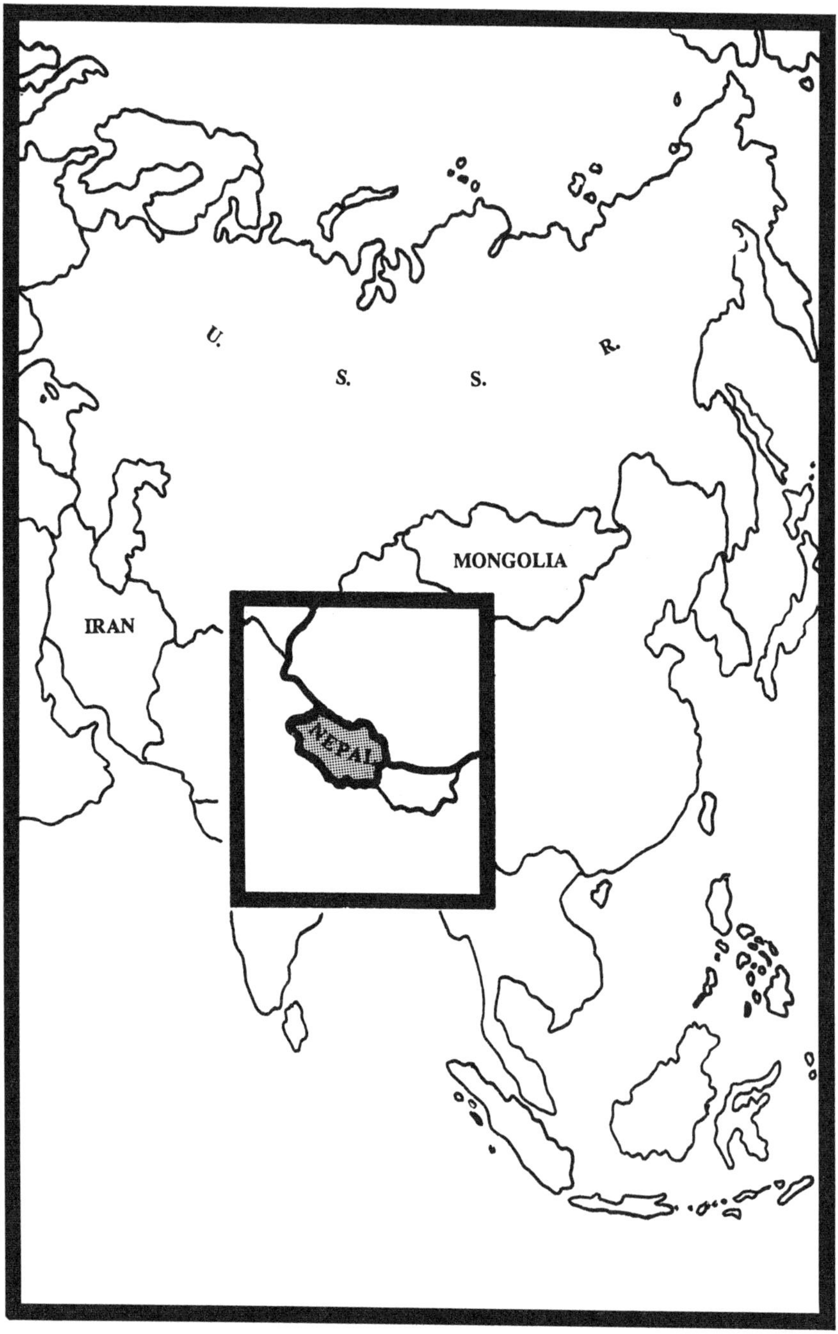
U.
S.
S.
R.
MONGOLIA
IRAN
NEPAL

Nepal

The primary religion in Nepal is Hindu. Religious tolerance is traditional, and constitutional guarantees provide for religious freedom. However, there is also a constitutional ban on conversion from one religion to another. Any Hindu who converts to another religion is subject to a year in jail, and those who proselytize a Hindu may be jailed for from three to six years. There were nine new cases of violating this law in 1986. Twenty-seven persons were charged with conversion and seventeen were charged with proselytizing. In Sirsia, a Catholic priest, two nuns and several Catholic laymen were arrested and charged under the proselytizing law. They claimed that they had only been ministering to Catholics in the area, and complained of maltreatment during their arrest and transfer to the capital. This incident marks only one of a number of occasional allegations by the Christians of harassment. A British/American human rights group visited Nepal in early 1986 to investigate some charges of persecution of Christians, and the government did investigate the Sirsia incident.

In 1984, forty Nepalese Christians from the western part of the country were arrested under the conversion and proselytization laws.

In 1989 four more people were sent to prison for converting from Hinduism to Christianity.

A number of Christian organizations operate schools, hospitals and other social service facilities, and foreign clergy are allowed to live and work in the country. However, the government has made it clear that open proselytizing would result in expulsion from the country.

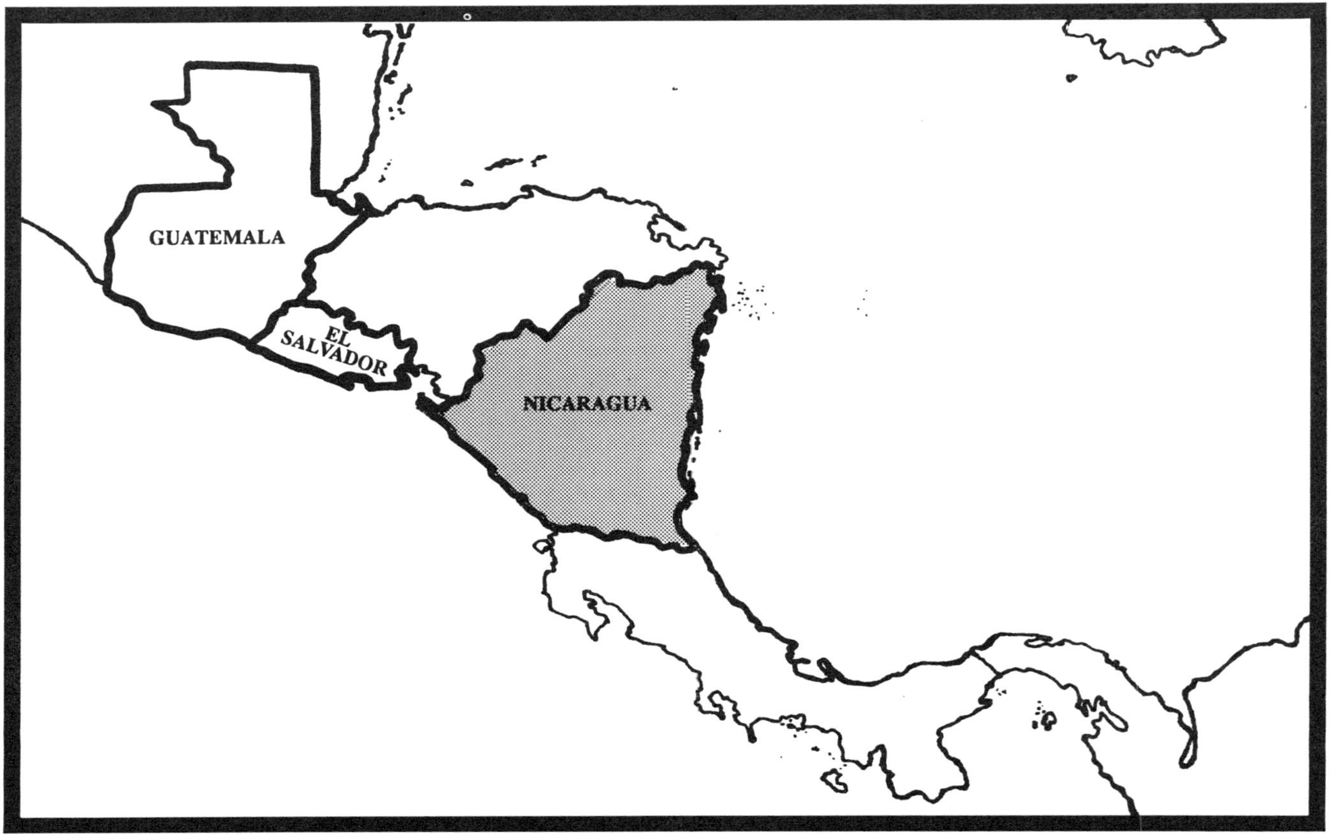
GUATEMALA
EL SALVADOR
NICARAGUA

Nicaragua

The majority of the Nicaraguan people are Christians, eighty-five percent Catholic. The government generally only practices retribution against those believers who are critical and vocal opponents of the government. Evangelicals and Catholic charismatics are the primary groups who seem to suffer for this reason.

The Catholic church is a primary defender of the human rights of Nicaraguans. Thus, there has been a steady assault on its institutions. In the winter of 1985, numerous reports were received of interrogation and imprisonment of Catholic lay workers. Juan Torrente, a Catholic activist, was arrested in December of 1985 and died in early 1986 of complications received from the beatings while he was in jail. Dozens of Catholic priests were interrogated and harassed, and several reported that they were physically abused. In November of 1985, Norman Talavera, the religion editor of *La Prensa*, was arrested and interrogated for five days about his relations with Cardinal Miguel Obando Bravo, and his involvement with the Catholic church. Two other church lay officials were also arrested.

The cardinal was twice denied permission to celebrate Mass. In January 1986, the Catholic radio facilities were permanently closed in an armed raid. In October of 1987, the Catholic radio station was allowed to reopen, but within less than three weeks was informed that it could not broadcast news programs. One of the archdiocesan commissions was declared an illicit organization. Cardinal Miguel Obando y Bravo has repeatedly stood up against the Sandinistas. He has warned that "Marxism does not have the solution for the working class." He has also insisted that the church, while obligated to take moral positions, must refrain from active political engagement. Cardinal Obando was born to Indian peasant parents in the south-central part of the country. He joined the Salesian order and became known as a priest to the poor. He rode through rough country on horseback to visit the impoverished backwoods villages. He has remained a humble man in spite of his church status and his increased stature resulting from showdowns with the government.

In 1986, the government-controlled media mounted a harsh campaign against the church hierarchy. Father Bismarck Carballo and Bishop Pablo Antonio Vega, the country's second-ranking Roman Catholic churchman, were expelled from the country, although President Daniel Ortega announced in September of 1987 that they would be able to return. An American priest was denied reentry after a visit to relatives in the United States, and his residence permit was confiscated. He was finally allowed to return after intervention from a number of church authorities. Father Gregorio Landaverde Flores, a Salvadoran priest and longtime resident of Nicaragua, was denied reentry when he returned from studies in Colombia.

The government on at least two occasions attempted to place priests in sexually embarrassing situations to discredit the church hierarchy. In 1982, such an attempt was made against church spokesman Monsignor Bismarck Carballo, and in 1984 against a visiting Venezuelan bishop and two priests.

In 1986, a number of attacks were made on Evangelicals and other Protestant denominations. In August, an Assembly of God church under construction in Managua was stormed and completely destroyed. Later, church officials were warned that they were prohibited indefinitely from conducting religious services.

Over three hundred Evangelicals were reported detained in the government's counterinsurgency campaign.

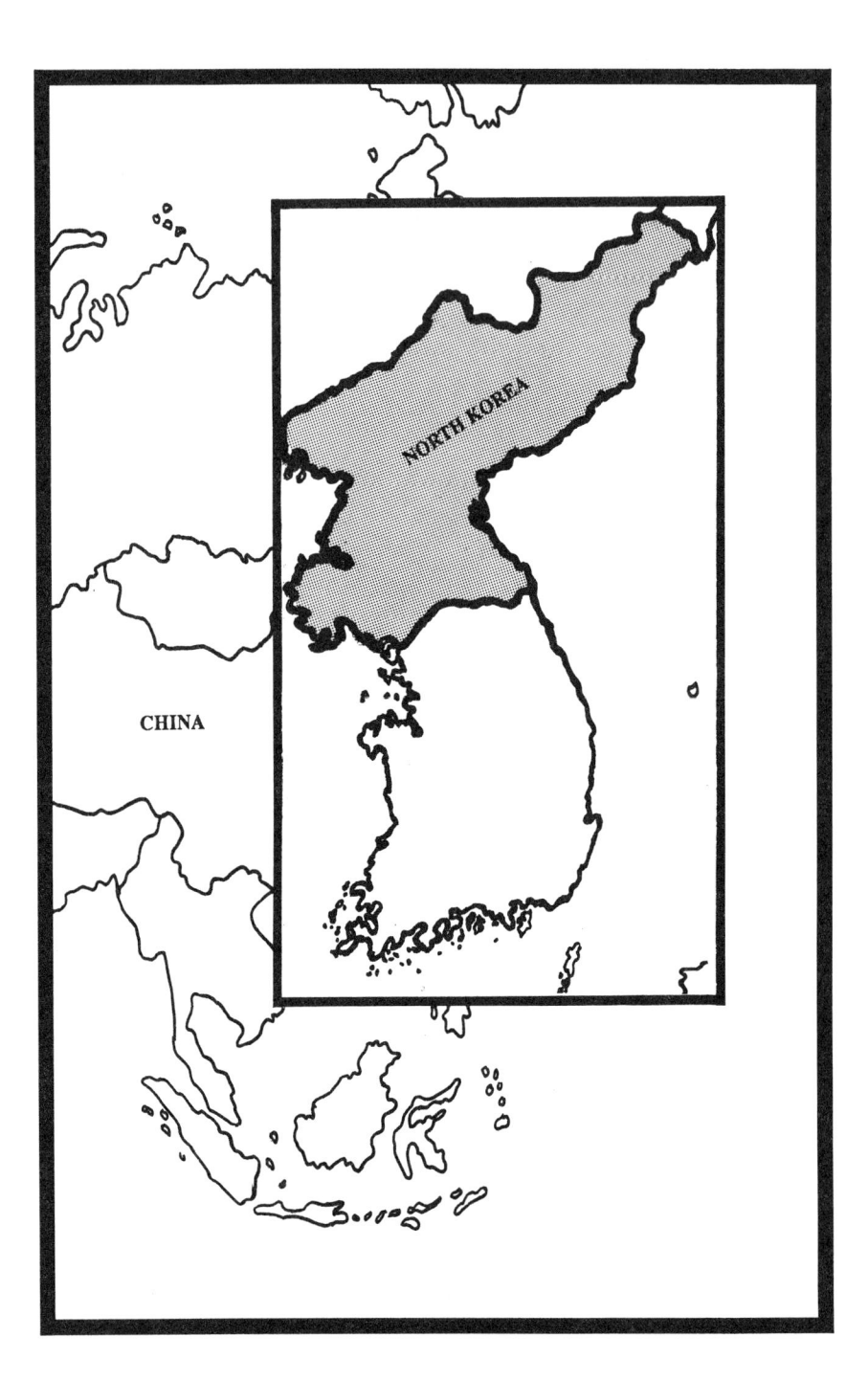

NORTH KOREA

CHINA

North Korea

(Democratic People's Republic of Korea)

North Korea has severely persecuted Christians since the 1940's. No churches have been rebuilt since the Korean War, and public worship is strictly prohibited. Apparently, the government is not currently persecuting the small number of Christians who worship at home. There is active discrimination against those whose relatives were known to have had a strong religious affiliation. Although the government has used religious organizational facades to proclaim the practice of religious freedom, it is doubtful if the original memberships have been retained. The constitution provides for religious liberty, but practice is not, apparently, in line with the constitutional guarantees.

ESTONIA
LATVIA
LITHUANIA
GERMAN DEMOCRATIC REPUBLIC
POLAND
CZECHOSLOVAKIA
HUNGARY
ROMANIA
YUGOSLAVIA
BULGARIA

Poland

Of the communist-bloc countries, Poland has been one of the most open. Polish citizens, under a constitutional guarantee of freedom of "conscience and belief," have been free to practice and worship, although the open practice of religion by party members has been discouraged by party officials.

After a period in which the Solidarity movement was outlawed, 1989 saw its stunning ascendancy to power, with the communists no longer in total control. Although the communists relinquished some control, they were also handing over an economy in a shambles. While the future bodes well for religious freedom in Poland, the new government is off to a difficult start, and a change of power in the future is not out of the question.

Catholicism is the major religion in Poland, and the church operates over 3,300 churches, schools and other institutions. New churches are being built, with the government's permission. One of the gains made by the Solidarity movement is the right to have religious services broadcast, and both the Catholic church and an independent Catholic press actively publish a number of works. Relations between the Catholic church and the government were strained during the first part of 1986, but an amnesty for political prisoners in September 1986 lessened the tensions somewhat.

Catholics in Poland campaign vigorously for greater individual freedoms and respect for all human rights, and the government and the government-controlled press have often been critical of what they consider unwarranted church interference in political affairs. They have often charged that the churches have been used to cover up political activities. Father Jerzy Popieluszko, who was kidnapped and murdered by the Polish police in 1984, was one of the most frequent targets of this type of accusation in the press.

In early 1987, Polish Cardinal Josef Glemp was interviewed in a leading Soviet newspaper, the weekly *Literaturnaja Gazeta*, which has led some to hope for a new and more positive phase in relations between Moscow and the Catholic church. No Soviet publication had previously carried an interview with the head of the Polish church, and speculation is that this might foreshadow a change in relations between Moscow and the pope.

In June of 1987, Pope John Paul II visited his homeland. In speech after speech, he challenged the government's policies in practically every aspect of social life. Frequently he pointed out that Christian faith must be lived publicly, in society and in daily work. He encouraged a patient struggle for human rights, and asked the faithful not to grow tired in their fight. During his trip, he seemed to demonstrate that the church does not pay for dialogue and diplomacy with silence on social issues.

In October 1987, American Vice President George Bush visited Warsaw. In company with Solidarity leader Lech Walesa, Bush traveled to St. Stanislaw Kostka church to visit the grave of Father Jerzy Popieluszko, an outspoken critic of the Polish government and a supporter of Solidarity. In his remarks, Bush said, "His soul is in the hands of God, but his spirit lives on in the people of Poland and the world."

* * *

With tears in his eyes, his voice breaking, the priest directed the congregation, "Repeat after me," as for the third time he spoke the line from the Lord's prayer, "as we forgive those who trespass against us." At last, the line was repeated with enormous force by the voices of the congregation at the packed vigil at St. Stanislaw's church in Warsaw. It was October 30, 1984, and the death of their beloved Father Jerzy Popieluszko had just been announced. The congregation was holding a prayer vigil in hopes that the priest had not been killed and that he would be returned safely. He had been missing since his abduction on the night of October 19. Panic, grief, and shock followed the finding of the battered corpse of the priest. The body was pulled from a reservoir on the river Vistula, about eighty miles northwest of Warsaw. The priest had been tortured, and the body was beyond recognition. A sack of rocks had been hung from the legs, and the body had been tied with a nylon rope so that if he had resisted Father Jerzy would have strangled himself. The corpse had been gagged, and the body was covered head to foot with deep, bloody wounds and marks of torture. The face was deformed, the hands were broken and cut, the eyes and forehead had been beaten and the jaw, nose, mouth and skull were smashed. Part of the scalp and large strips of skin on the legs had been torn off. When Father Jerzy's mouth was opened, all of the teeth were found to be completely smashed.

One of the doctors who performed the post-mortem reported that he had never seen anyone so mutilated internally. Identification from a birthmark on the side of his chest was finally made by the priest's brother.

Of what crime was this fragile, defenseless priest accused? Officially, none. Why was he kidnapped, horribly tortured, and murdered? Father Jerzy Popieluszko preached and lived a defense of basic human rights, a song of freedom.

"One must suffer for the truth. That is why I am ready for anything," Father Jerzy had written to Pope John Paul II. At his last Mass, a special Mass for the Working People in the provincial town of Bydgoszcz, Father Jerzy preached a final sermon that exemplified all he stood for, "Overcome Evil with Good." His last words to the congregation were, "Most of all, may we be free from the desire for violence and vengeance." In the spirit of his words, the congregation at his vigil prayed, "as we forgive those who trespass against us." On the day of his funeral, ten thousand steelworkers in hard hats marched past secret-police headquarters. One of the slogans they chanted over and over was "We forgive." Jerzy Popieluszko was born in 1947 in Okopy, a small hamlet in eastern Poland about twenty miles from the Soviet border. His parents were poor farmers. The family of six lived in a small two-room house with only a stove for heat. As a child, Jerzy was in chronic ill health. Friends recall him as self-effacing, always doing things for others. Before school, he would rise early and walk three miles to serve as an altar boy at the nearest church. He was a loner, nicknamed "the philosopher" for his habit of being caught up in his own thoughts. He loved Polish history, and, even in the state-run schools he attended, he spoke his mind. Saint Maximilian Kolbe was one of Jerzy's heroes, and after high school Jerzy attended a seminary in Warsaw in order to be close to the monastery that Kolbe had created.

After a happy first year at the seminary, Jerzy was drafted into a special army-indoctrination unit in 1966. Here he became the spiritual leader of his unit. For leading prayer services, Jerzy was assigned extra-hard labor. He was forced to crawl around the camp like a dog because he recited the rosary to brain-washing specialists. When an officer found him with a rosary, he demanded that Jerzy renounce his faith. The young seminarian refused, so he was beaten severely and put in isolation for a month. In a letter to his father describing the ordeal, Jerzy wrote, "I have turned out to be very tough. I can't be broken by threats or torture." The stay at the indoctrination unit ruined his health, although Jerzy told one of his seminary masters, "One doesn't suffer when one suffers for Christ."

After his ordination in 1972, Jerzy was appointed chaplain to Warsaw's medical students and nurses. Everyone admired his readiness to be with people in all circumstances, his easygoing nature, and his courage. Though he tried to hide it, his illness was taking its toll, and his fainting spells became more frequent. One day while saying Mass, Father Jerzy fell unconscious. He was suffering from a serious blood disorder that would require transfusions with each recurrence. A quiet life and a special diet would help prevent further deterioration from the disease, so in June of 1980 he was assigned to the parish of St. Stanislaw Kostka near the huge Warsaw steelworks.

Despite threats from the Kremlin, the Polish workers stood united and Solidarity was born. By the end of August 1980, the Polish people had won the unprecedented right to free trade unions and some other key reforms. The steelworkers wanted to celebrate Mass, and although other clergymen had refused their request to come to the plant, Father Jerzy heard their call and came. The first priest to enter the factory, the frail young Father Popieluszko said Mass for a group of tired men in grimy overalls, who knelt on the concrete to receive communion.

A peasant's son, Jerzy Popieluszko knew work and workers. His straight talk and his cheerful dedication impressed the workers, who listened as he spoke about overcoming evil with good. He reminded them, "We are created to be free, free as God's children." He calmed the hotheads and blessed the long line of men. Soon the men realized that the young priest would stay by them, and affectionately began to call him Jurek. At last, when the exhausted thousands of workers ended their historic strike, Father Jerzy made a vow, "to stay among my workers as long as I can." In honoring this vow, he became the most popular priest in Poland, and the spiritual patron of the Solidarity movement. He vowed to stay, and stay he did. After his death, pressure was brought by the authorities to bury the martyr priest in his home village, far away from Warsaw and the workers. This was in hopes that the priest, as a symbol of freedom, would be forgotten sooner. Father Jerzy's mother, along with a delegation of workers, went to Cardinal Glemp, the Polish primate, and on her knees she pleaded, "The shepherd should be where his lambs are."

Father Jerzy loved the steel mill and its workers. "My whole strategy is the dignity of human labor and the struggle with hatred," he said. He wanted the workers to recover the spirit of pride, honor, and dignity that the state had denied them. During the fifteen months of Solidarity's partial freedom, the secret police constantly shadowed the dangerous little priest. In October of 1981, Father Jerzy went to America for the funeral of one of his cousins. American friends asked him to stay and take political asylum. He replied, "My people will be in danger if I abandon them. They need me and I need them."

When the Solidarity movement was forced underground, Father Jerzy accepted it as a challenge to be with his people "in their days of trial." After martial law was imposed, he became busier than ever, attending to the temporal as well as the spiritual needs of his parishioners. From the rectory, he ran the center that distributed medical aid to all of Warsaw, and people came from far away to give him aid for the victims of repression. One woman asked him, "How can I take help from the church? My husband and I aren't even believers."

"That doesn't matter now. We are divided only into people who need and people who can give," the courageous priest answered.

Commenting on Father Jerzy's constant concern for others, Solidarity leader Lech Walesa said, "He really didn't care about himself."

Martial law silenced millions of Poles, but Father Jerzy would not remain silent. The political trials of the workers inspired him to begin a monthly Mass for the Homeland, dedicated to all of the victims of the regime's harsh policies. This Mass grew into a national event, and Poles came from all parts of the country to attend. He said, "[You] will rise again after any humiliation, for you have knelt only before God." Constantly he repeated, "Overcome evil with good." When he preached against fear, it enraged the government for it threatened the state's most effective weapon.

Father Jerzy received threatening letters and death warnings. After one particularly vicious threat, he told a friend, "The most they can do is kill me." In December of 1982, a first attempt on his life was made. He had just gone to bed when his doorbell rang. He was too tired to get up, and in a few moments, a bomb crashed into the next room, exploding where he would have been standing had he gone to answer the door. The state media began propaganda attacks against Father Jerzy.

In December of 1983, he was arrested on trumped-up charges, and taken to jail briefly. He was released after church-state negotiations. The incident did seem to create a problem with Cardinal Glemp, and there were rumors that he was preparing to transfer Father Jerzy. At this time, two messages arrived from Rome. The pope sent Father Jerzy a rosary with his blessing. Father kept this rosary until the end. The pope also sent a message to the cardinal: "Defend Father Popieluszko—or they'll start finding weapons in the desk of every second bishop."

Some students had given Father Jerzy a little black puppy. His name for this pet was "Tajniak" (Polish for "secret agent") because the puppy followed him everywhere.

Death threats by phone and letter began to increase and grow more alarming. In the first half of 1984, Father Jerzy was called to thirteen interrogations, staged to terrorize him. A group of supporters always accompanied him to secret-police headquarters, waiting outside, chanting hymns and prayers until the end of the ordeal. Inside, with his hands behind his back, Father Jerzy would finger the rosary the pope had sent him. His interrogators' ruthless questions were answered by reciting the rosary, again and again. At last the furious authorities would release him.

Father Jerzy remained determined to preach. He told an Italian journalist, "If I shut up, it means they have won. To speak out is precisely my job."

On October 13, 1984, another attempt was made on Father Jerzy's life. Thanks to the quick reflexes of his driver-bodyguard,

Waldemar Chrostowski, the car in which they were riding was able to elude the secret-police ambush. On Friday, October 19, Father Jerzy spoke at a special Mass for the Working People. Secret agents waited outside. Father Jerzy was very ill and barely able to speak. He and Chrostowski left Bydgoszcz to return to Warsaw. About a half hour from Bydgoszcz, the secret police overtook the priest and his driver. The driver was held at gunpoint, while the kidnappers beat the priest with fists and clubs. Unconscious, he was bound, gagged, and thrown into the trunk. An ex-commando, Chrostowski was able to hurl himself out of the car in a desperate escape. He made it to a nearby workers' hostel and quickly raised an alarm. With his escape, news of the abduction quickly spread across Poland. The nation's churches were filled with people for twenty-four-hour vigils, and the nation's workers prayed and hoped for the life of their priest.

The last Sunday of October, a record 50,000 people engulfed St. Stanislaw's for an outdoor Mass for the Homeland. While listening to a tape of his last sermon, they hoped against hope to see Father Jerzy again.

At last, the fateful word came. The state held an unusual trial, and, as the assassins had feared, they were thrown to the lions to protect their higher-ups.

On the day of Father Jerzy's funeral, half a million people filled the streets leading up to the parish church of St. Stanislaw. The country stood united again around its heroic martyr priest. Overnight the church became a mighty national shrine. Since his death, new converts have flooded into Polish churches. Many who had lapsed have returned. His murder has given courage to many priests, and his example is inspiring vocations to the priesthood.

Although there were hopes that the trial of Father Jerzy's killers might mark a change in policy, the persecution of priests has continued. Torture and unexplained deaths of priests are still a practice. Jan Watroba, an outspoken vicar and Piotr Poplawski, an Orthodox priest, have both died in suspicious circumstances.

Fr. Jerzy Popielusko. Photo courtesy of Pauline Fathers, National Shrine of Our Lady of Czestochowa.

GERMAN DEMOCRATIC REPUBLIC
POLAND
CZECHOSLOVAKIA
HUNGARY
ROMANIA
YUGOSLAVIA
BULGARIA

Romania

The bloody revolution that deposed Ceaucescu as leader of Romania has given observers cause for both hope and alarm—hope because the communists have lost power; alarm because of the ethnic strife that in part led to the violence of the revolution. Until the revolution, the government of Romania officially recognized fourteen denominations, and exercised broad power over them through the Department of Religious Affairs. The state issued licenses to preach, and permits to construct churches, and rigorously controlled the importation and printing of religious materials.

The state espoused atheism, and discrimination in job advancement of believers did exist. Constitutional religious freedom existed as well, and religious activity was and is widespread. State-controlled media, however, portrayed believers as stupid and backward.

The evangelical denominations have grown rapidly, and there is a shortage of Protestant Bibles, which caused some to risk heavy penalties in attempting to smuggle these into the country. In 1986, a number of religious activists were released from prison and allowed to emigrate. These included three Baptist pastors.

One positive recent development was the agreement by the authorities to allow a new printing of Bibles, the first since the 1920's. On the other hand, permits for church construction and repair were consistently denied, and seminary applications were severely restricted.

The Roman Catholic church was technically without an approved government charter because of disagreement with the government on a number of issues. It operated, however, as if it were fully recognized.

Romanian criminal law was written in broad terms, thus ensuring that persons who came under government disapproval could easily be convicted of some crime. A person found attempting to hand out free Bibles could easily have been convicted of the felony of "distributing literature without a license."

In 1984, there were fewer cases reported of harassment, although the persecution of members of churches not recognized by the state continued. Individuals were still being fined and imprisoned for religious practices. In early 1984, a Baptist minister was arrested and fined for worshiping in private homes. Father Gheorghe Calciu, a Romanian Orthodox priest, was released from prison in August 1984. He had been imprisoned since 1979 for sermons critical of the government. In the spring of 1984, a Pentecostal church in Cluj-Napoca was demolished because of unauthorized remodeling of the interior. The largest Baptist church in the country, in Oradea, was ordered demolished due to the redevelopment of the area where it was located. In 1985, a few Catholic clergy were allowed to travel abroad for training and consultations.

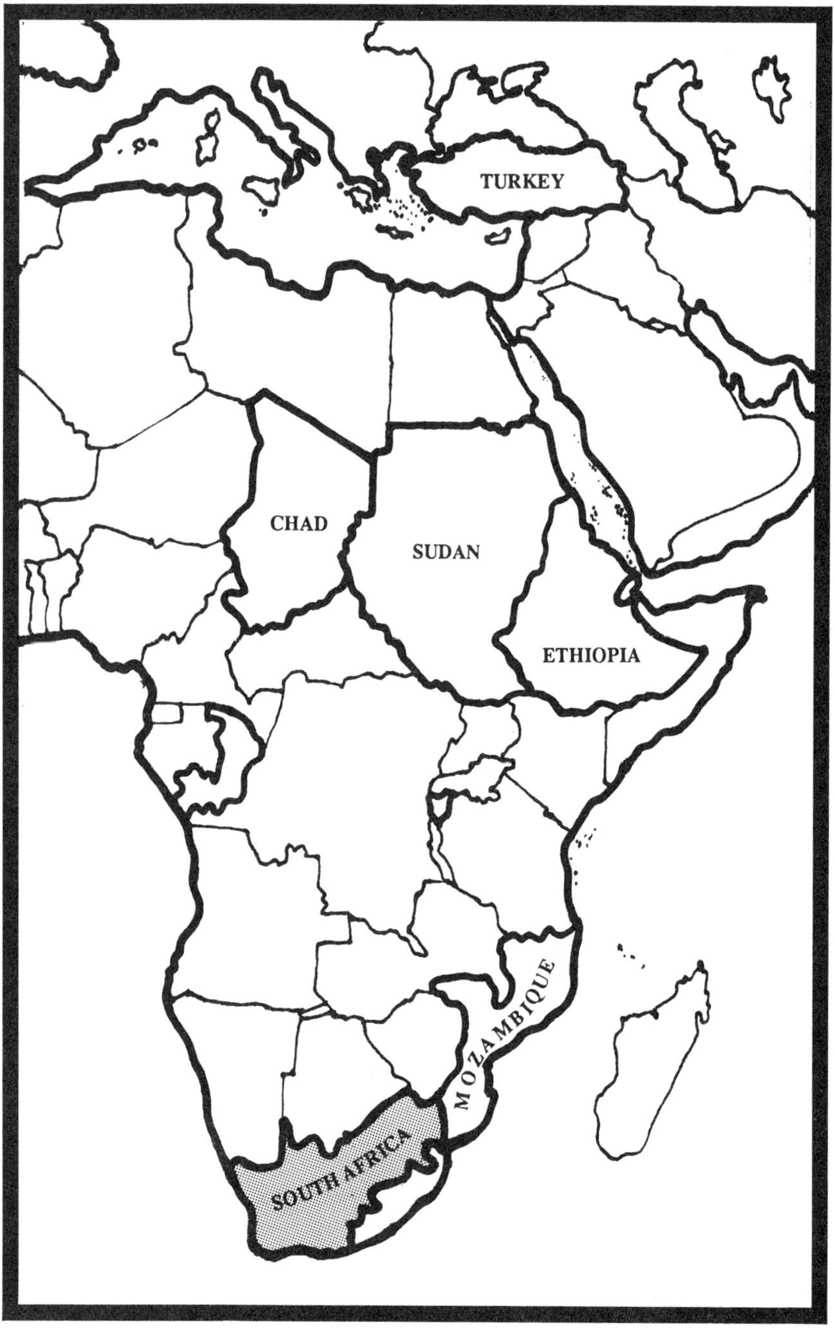
TURKEY
CHAD
SUDAN
ETHIOPIA
MOZAMBIQUE
SOUTH AFRICA

South Africa

Although the government of South Africa generally respects freedom of worship, the government was often at odds with religious leaders in 1986. This was due to their criticism of the country's system of racial segregation, apartheid. Among these were Catholic Archbishop Denis Hurley of Durban; the Anglican Archbishop of Cape Town, Desmond Tutu; and the Reverend Allan Boesak, President of the World Alliance of Reformed Churches. In November, the government dropped charges of subversion that had been pending against Rev. Boesak for over a year. He had made an effort to stage a protest march near Poolsmoor prison in Cape Town where ANC leader Nelson Mandela was imprisoned.

Churchmen have sometimes been detained, often without criminal charges. Dean Simon Farisani of the Evangelical Lutheran church was detained in Venda in late November of 1986, and remained in detention in early 1987. Also in November of that year, an American citizen missionary, Larry Hill, was detained for two weeks without charges. Another American, Marianhill Father James Paulsen, was detained in December.

The South African Council of Churches is often criticized by government ministers, and was subjected to an investigation in 1984. In spite of the critical tone of the report of this investigation, the government has not taken overt action against the organization.

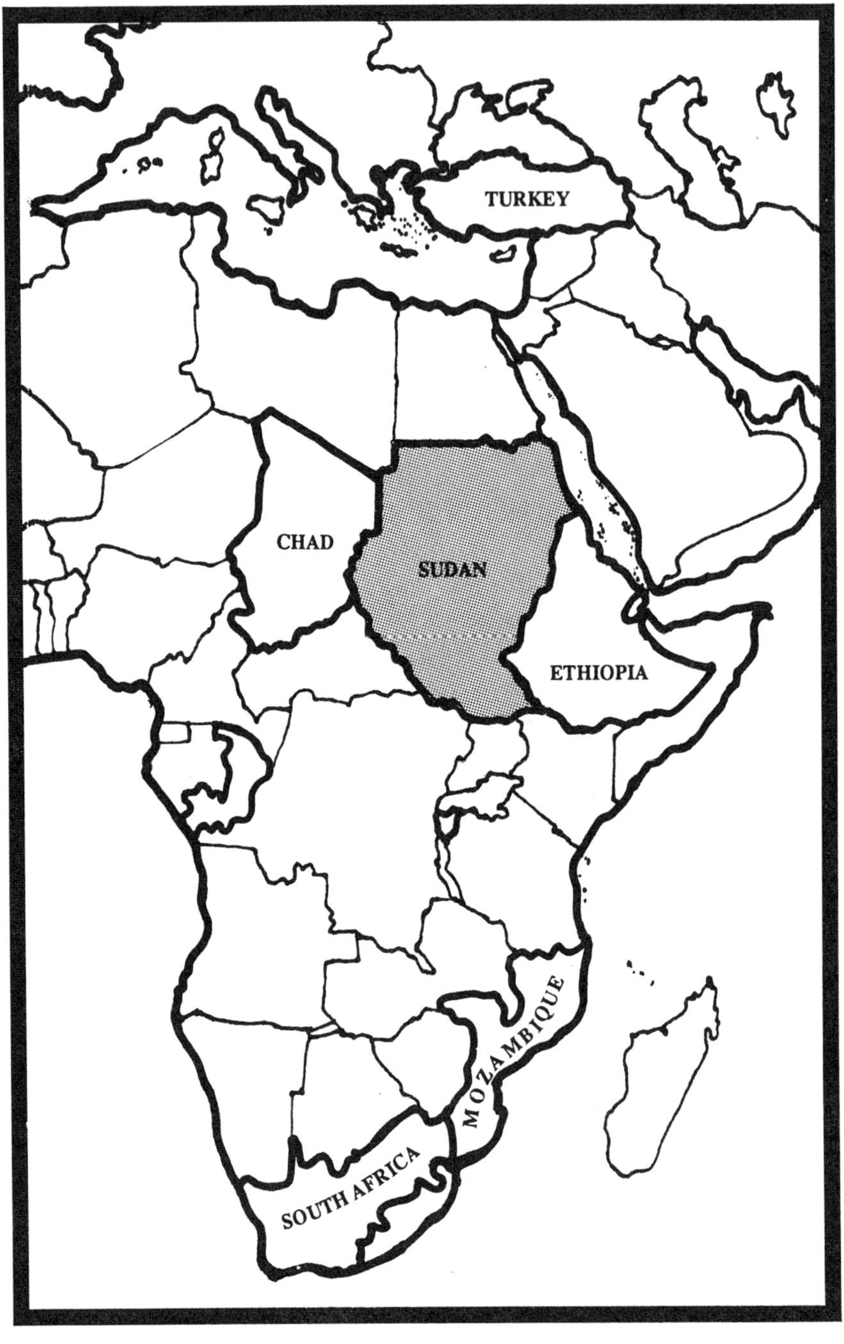
TURKEY
CHAD
SUDAN
ETHIOPIA
MOZAMBIQUE
SOUTH AFRICA

Sudan

Christian missionaries are active in Sudan, but they claim that they may not preach to Muslims, and three people were arrested in 1986 for doing so. Although Christian denominations are growing, the government has refused to issue them new building permits. This forces the churches to preach in overcrowded churches built in colonial times, or outside, which requires them to obtain an assembly permit. Some Christian groups have also had difficulty obtaining permits to do relief work. Father Jebrayil Tutu, a Nubian Anglican priest, was arrested on suspicion of aiding an opposition political force in May 1985. He was cruelly tortured while being questioned. His hands were so tightly tied that he has lost the use of them, and he is still recovering from serious burns due to being left tied to metal pipes in the sun during the day.

Christian-Muslim relations in the Nubian areas of southern Sudan have historically been uneasy, and tensions reached a new high in early 1986. Sixteen Christian churches in South Kordofan were closed in early 1986 by order of the authorities. A number of local churchmen and residents were arrested for disobeying the order. An Italian priest in Kadugli was arrested and charged with inciting the people against the government. In the same area, two clinics run by Italian priests and nuns were closed. Four churches were burned by "persons unknown."

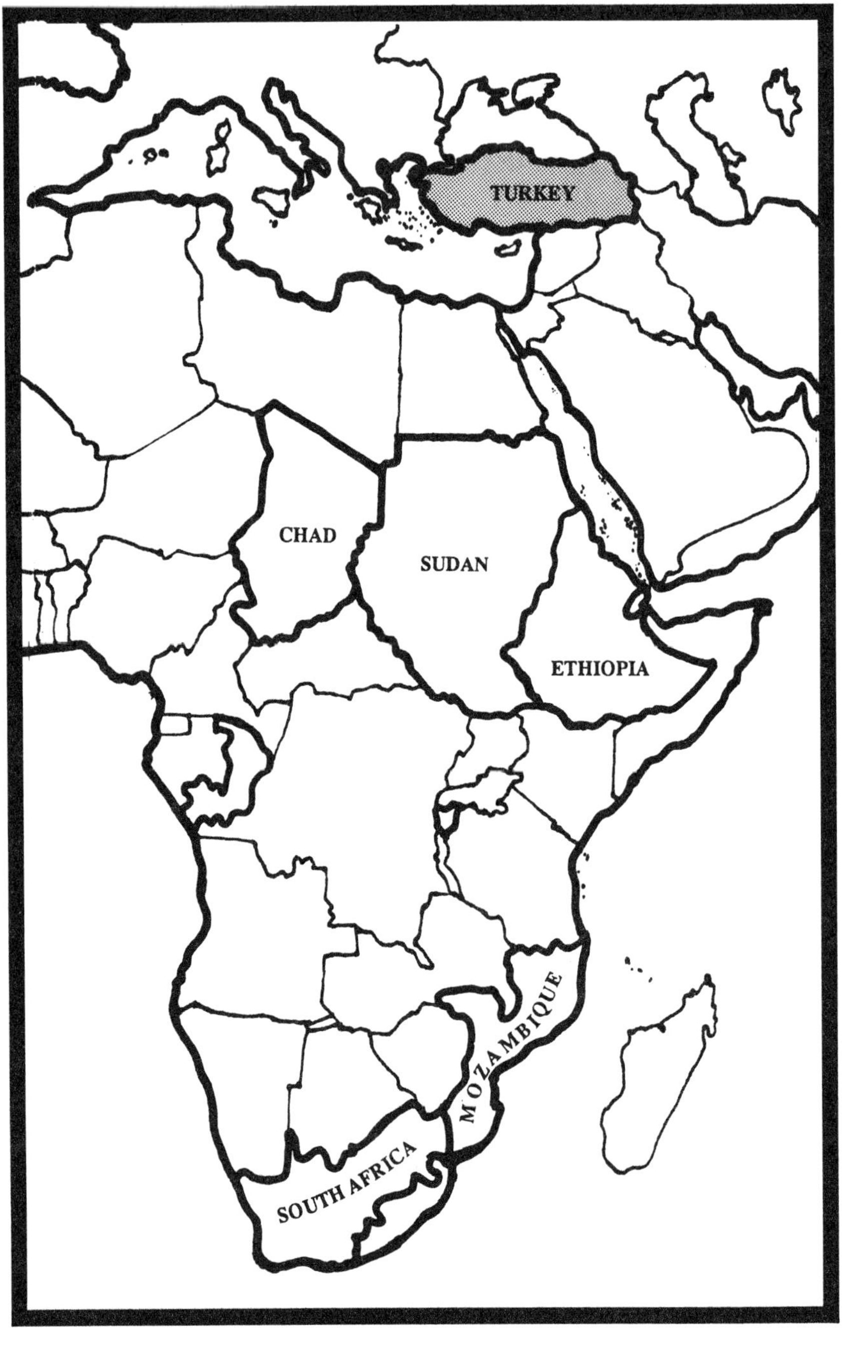

TURKEY
CHAD
SUDAN
ETHIOPIA
MOZAMBIQUE
SOUTH AFRICA

Turkey

The Turkish constitution states that all have the right to religious freedom. However, laws aimed at upholding secularism and the separation of church and state make significant limits on that right.

The Criminal Code forbids proselytizing by anyone. A recent court decision in favor of the Jehovah's Witnesses upheld the constitutional freedom of religion, and is seen as a positive sign.

In late 1985, Istanbul police confiscated Turkish publications belonging to the Turkish Bible Society, but these were released in the spring of 1986 after intervention by the prime minister.

Turkey is primarily a Muslim country, although small numbers of Armenian Orthodox and Catholic, Greek Orthodox and Catholic, Roman Catholic, Syrian and Assyrian Christian, Protestants and Jewish believers are found in the country, primarily around Istanbul. A number of Christian groups have objected to a mandate from the Department of Education that all children attend classes in the Muslim beliefs, and some parts of the classes have been modified for non-Muslims. In 1986, the government took a number of steps to improve relations with the non-Muslim minorities.

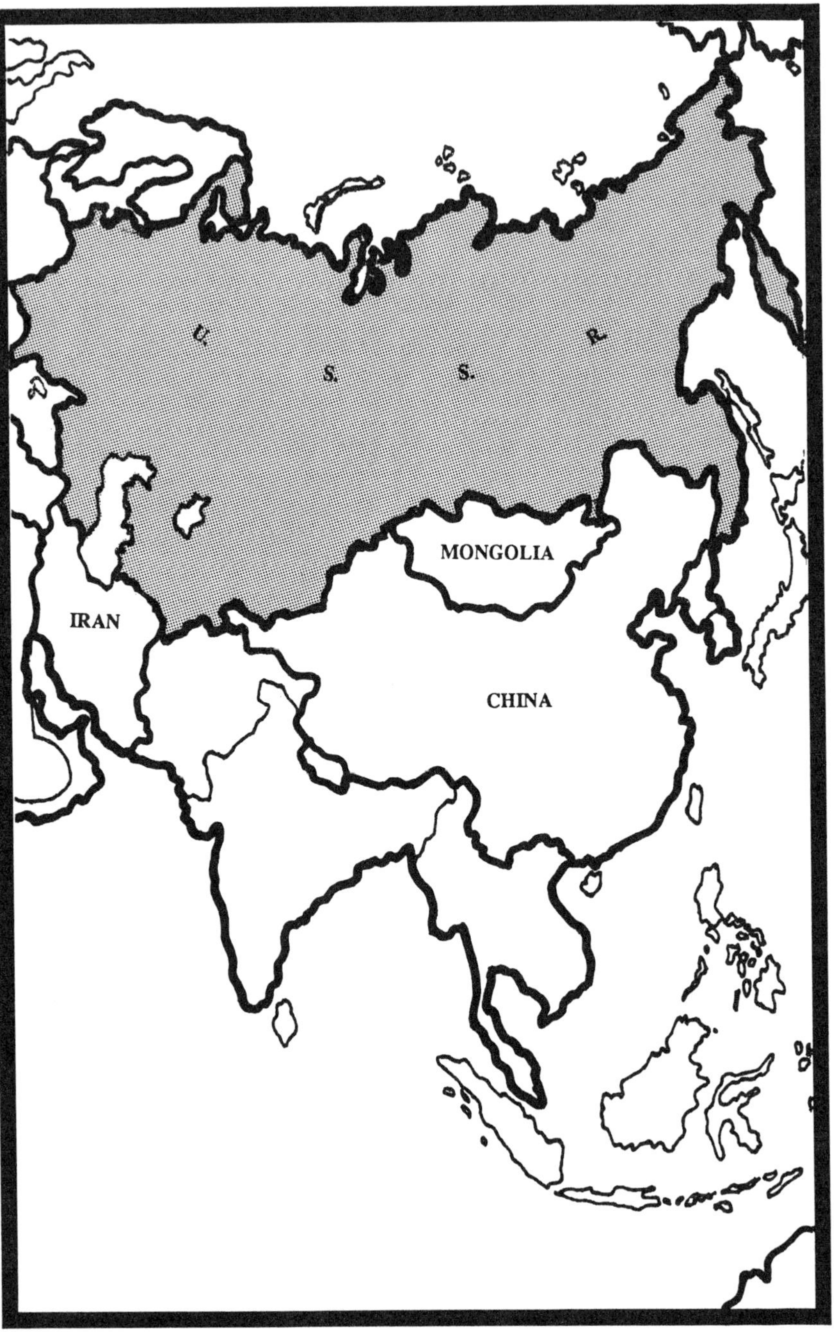
U.
S.
S.
R.
MONGOLIA
IRAN
CHINA

Union of Soviet Socialist Republics

While the much-heralded glasnost and perestroika have definitely resulted in a loosening of restrictions on religious practice, and the communist grip on the government has been relaxing, as of early 1990 there are still serious problems for practicing Christians in Soviet society. The organization Aid to the Church in Need reported that, even under perestroika, priests were still persecuted, people were not allowed to pray freely or openly, church weddings and funerals were forbidden, and religious assemblies were viewed as illegal gatherings. In 1989, Anna Tapay wrote in the *National Catholic Register,* "There's evidence that Moscow is merely becoming more nuanced at suppressing dissent and persecuting religious believers. Instead of arresting, publicly prosecuting and then sentencing dissidents to long periods of imprisonment, the Soviets have begun a practice of repeated short-term detention.

The USSR's domination of much of Europe and Asia make the status of the church there a weathervane for measuring the likelihood of continued reforms elsewhere. At this writing, the USSR has yet to fully emerge from its long and bloody history of religious persecution, which has been without regard for religious denomination.

In the officially atheistic state, all adherents to a belief in God have been equally subject to harassment and persecution. Soviet Jews have shared in this along with their Christian brethren.

Because of the way the constitutional guarantee of the freedom of religion is worded, and because of additional extensive legislation and government regulations, the government has exercised a great deal of control and restriction of religion in the USSR. All religious groups of twenty or more have had to register with the Soviet Council of Religious Affairs. This council's refusal to grant legal status has been used against the Ukrainian Catholic (Uniate) church since 1946.

After registration, there have been regulations against proselytizing, Bible study groups, charitable activities, religious discussions and formal religious instruction for children. Some children have been removed from families who permit this type of instruction instead of Soviet schooling. Participation in religious services has been cause for exclusion from the communist party, and party membership is necessary for educational and career advancement, so believers have effectively been discriminated against in this manner. Seminaries and ministerial schools are small and entrance to them has been strictly regulated; thus there is insufficient clergy for the recognized groups. Only a few officially controlled religious publications have been permitted. The printing and importation of Bibles and other printed religious materials have been strictly controlled by the state. In spite of all these restrictions, the government has acknowledged that up to 70 million Soviet citizens adhere to some religion.

Many religious groups have refused to register, as some of the laws contradict tenets of their beliefs. These persons have been harassed at school and at work, and denied access to housing. Some have been dismissed from work or imprisoned. One Western source recently listed approximately four hundred religious activists serving prison sentences on charges relating to their beliefs. The unregistered Pentecostals have suffered severe persecutions. Two Baptists who had already spent time in prison were resentenced in 1986 to longer terms. In mid-1987, over a hundred Baptists remained in labor camps, according to statistics from Keston College.

The largest traditional church is the Russian Orthodox. Although this church has been tolerated, the authorities have discouraged the population's interest and have called for more atheistic education. Believers who are active in other than officially sanctioned church rituals are punished. A number of Orthodox activists were sentenced to prison and to labor camps in 1986.

In the Ukraine, defenders of the outlawed Uniate church have remained active. A new crackdown by the government began against the group during the last half of 1984. One priest was arrested and two of his colleagues were detained and threatened. A Catholic church near Lvov was burned and two monasteries were closed. These actions followed the appearance of a samizdat (self-published) journal, *The Chronicle of the Catholic Church in the Ukraine.* In 1985, Joseph Terelya and Vasiliy Kobrin, church leaders, were again imprisoned.

Catholic activists continued to be persecuted. Kirill Popov, a Moscow Catholic, was sentenced in April of 1986 to six years in labor camp and five years of exile. He was charged, among other things, with having "given moral and material support" to political prisoners. This charge had not been heard officially since Stalinist days.

Those who write, publish or distribute samizdat religious materials have been subject to severe reprisals, which have included warnings, loss of job, searches, arrest, conviction, or incarceration in a mental hospital. Six Baptist publishers in Moldavia were sentenced to two years in a labor camp in May 1986. The government often has placed selected political and religious activists in psychiatric hospitals, where they have been subjected to the painful, forced administration of sedatives, antipsychotics and other drugs. Catholic activist Aleksandr Riga was sentenced to indefinite treatment in a special psychiatric hospital for promoting religious practices among friends and disseminating religious material.

In 1986, a number of reports of death under unusual circumstances of people engaged in religious dissent were brought forward. Official involvement in such deaths cannot be proved or investigated. A number of prisoners have died each year in prison or forced-labor camps because of the severe conditions. So many Soviet prisoners have suffered both mental and physical abuse and mistreatment during interrogation, trial and confinement that this type of treatment is regarded as a systematic practice.

Prisoners have not been allowed to practice their religion and have been punished for attempts to do so.

In February 1987, over one hundred political prisoners were freed, including Joseph Terelya and Kirill Popov mentioned above, as well as fifteen other religious activists. A number of others had been freed in late 1986. These releases, however, by no means account for all of the political prisoners in the Soviet Union.

* * *

In 1944, the Soviets occupied the Carpathian region. Soviet authorities claimed that there was a "voluntary self-liquidation" of the Church Union in the Eparchy of Mukachevo, and denied the existence of the Byzantine Catholic church in the Carpathian and Subcarpathian regions. The church was forced underground and became known as the Church of Silence. Its members have actively worked for Soviet recognition and legalization. Periodically, the Soviets have renewed persecution of the Byzantine Catholics. In 1949, the Cathedral Church of Uzhorod and the Eparchial Administration Building were taken from the Byzantine Catholics and placed under the jurisdiction of the Russian Orthodox church. All Greek Catholic churches were ordered closed and the priests were forbidden to exercise their ministry unless approved by the Orthodox archbishop. One by one, the secret police called in the Greek Catholic priests and tried to "persuade" them to join the Orthodox church. By 1949, out of 340 active priests in the Mukachevo Eparchy, 18 had died during interrogations, 40 had died or been killed in prison camps, 147 who refused to sign over to Orthodoxy had been condemned to forced labor in Siberia, and 36 had been able to escape to the West. A vicious persecution of the Byzantine Catholic church had begun; it continued for years, and may not be over yet.

In spite of continuous repression and vicious propaganda, the people have remained true to their Catholic faith. The initiative in the attempt to legalize the Byzantine Catholic church was taken by a dedicated young artist and writer, Joseph Terelya of Dovhe, Irshava County, Subcarpathia. In the fall of 1982, he organized the "Promoting Group for the Defense of the Rights of Believers and the Church." For his activities, Joseph Terelya has himself been persecuted, incarcerated and forced into intensive labor. Nonetheless, his spirit is not broken, and he is determined to continue his efforts towards true religious freedom in the Soviet Union.

Joseph Terelya was born in 1943 in Subcarpathian Ruthenia (since 1945 incorporated into the Soviet Ukraine). His grandparents were devout Catholics, and from his early youth he became an active member of the Church of Silence. Terelya himself said that he enjoyed going to church with his grandmother, but soon his childish curiosity about religion became a "crime."

Shortly after his graduation from high school (Construction School) in 1962, he was imprisoned by the Soviet secret police (KGB) for his illegal religious activities, and tried and convicted for alleged "anti-Soviet activities." He was condemned to four years in a corrective labor camp. As soon as he set foot in the camp, he was searched. He was wearing a locket with a picture of the Blessed Virgin which was taken away from him. For having dared to bring this "overt propaganda" into the camp, he was given fifteen days of solitary confinement. Harassment and persecution were his lot here. One incident he recalled occurred on November 3, 1966. The captain brought Terelya and the other religious prisoners together. Then he told Terelya to undress, which he did. The captain then asked if it were true that Christians were baptized with water. He then forced Terelya to go, naked, out into the courtyard in front of the other prisoners. He handed him a Bible and the locket with the icon of the Blessed Mother that had been confiscated from him on his arrival in camp. Then the guards began to pour water over him, and jeer at him to be saved by the Almighty Jesus Christ. Those believers who began to cry and pray for Terelya were beaten immediately. Later, the believers were drenched with swill, which froze in the cold air and made ice over their bodies.

In 1972, Terelya was tried again, this time for writing his collection of poems entitled *Bitterness*. He was sent to a psychiatric prison hospital in Sychevka, and later to a special hospital in Dnipropetrovsk.

Terelya's description of conditions in the Sychevka prison hospital is horrifying. The orderlies, usually criminal offenders, would beat and otherwise mistreat the other political "psychos" for any reason at all. Packages mailed to the inmates were confiscated and searched. Sometimes, for laughs, the orderlies forced the political prisoners to eat live frogs. Often the inmates were raped by the orderlies. Some were beaten nightly until death. A Russian artist was hanged with the knowledge of the supervisors, who simply listed his death as a suicide. Between 1963 and 1973, a total of 475 inmates were killed or tortured to death. Terelya himself was punished for obtaining pencil and paper—first they broke the fingers on his hand and later tied him to the bed.

After his return in 1976, on September 21, Terelya was looking for work in Vinnytsa. He was seized by secret agents and told to leave their region. They took him to a cemetery after dark. He was hit and fell to the ground, then beaten unconscious. When he came to because of the cold, he was tied to a cross, and his mouth was gagged with a scarf. The agents told Terelya to "think about it" while they went to wet their throats. They left him tied to the cross in the cemetery until the night of November 23, when they released him. They warned him to keep silent about the incident, or they would again have him committed. A year later he was again incarcerated by the KGB. Because of the repeated intervention of his wife, he was finally released in the fall of 1981, and he returned home still determined to fight for human rights and religious freedom for his people. In the summer of 1982, Terelya organized the Promoting Group for the Defense of the Rights of Believers and the Church, which was shortly extended to Galicia, where the Byzantine Catholic church was also liquidated and placed outside the law by the Soviets in the 1940's.

In September of 1982, Terelya wrote a letter to the Central Committee of the Soviet Ukrainian Communist Party in Kiev, officially notifying them about the formation of the group and attempting to set forth his purely religious convictions, and to dispel the unfounded accusations of anti-Soviet activities. His determination to fight for the religious freedom of his people and the legalization of the Byzantine Catholic church in the Soviet Union is clearly shown in a letter of his that was smuggled to the Free World:

"On September 9, 1982, The Promoting Group for the Defense of the Rights of Believers and the Church was formed in the Ukraine. I was elected head of this Promoting Group, while Rev. Gregory Budzynsky was elected secretary. Two other priests, Father Dionysius and Father Ignatius, and a believer, Stephanie Petrash-Sichko, also joined the group. This was in response to the appeal of Byzantine Catholics concerning the increased repression of our Church. From this day forward, all information on the Byzantine Catholic church in the Ukraine will be brought to the attention of the world community. Catholics in the entire world must know and remember the circumstances in which we live.

"We have only one goal—legalization! To be equal with all other groups in the Soviet population. Despite the statements and prognosis of some Party members, we are living, growing, and overcoming all difficulties. The trials and persecution of the

Byzantine Catholics in the Ukraine have strengthened us further in our faith, and have given us the opportunity to sound the depths of God's work. I can state without exaggeration that there is nothing greater than to die in a Communist prison as a Byzantine Catholic, as one who has lost his fear and has found truth and hope. Therefore, we still believe that the Kingdom of God will come and will have no end.

"I have been charged with fanaticism and all kinds of violations by the unbelievers. Those who accuse me forget that the Catholic Church is a loving Church, a tolerant Church, and the universal Church. The idea of Jesus Christ is the most revolutionary idea in the course of the past twenty centuries. 'Christ died for us. We are justified by His blood' (Rom. 5:9-10), and we must remember this and live accordingly. Where the blood of the Savior is not acknowledged, there comes and must come destruction and death.

"Although the forces of evil are still strong today, we, Catholics, believe and know that all evil has its end as it had its beginning, since we live in times of constant upheavals. Therefore we confidently follow Him who told us: 'Take courage! I have overcome the world' (Jn. 16:33).

"[signed] Joseph Terelya"

Terelya knew that shortly after the letter was received he would probably be incarcerated again. Therefore, the Group immediately sent a memorandum to the Presidium of the Soviet Ukraine in Kiev requesting the restoration of the Byzantine Catholic church.

Almost immediately, Mr. Petrash-Sichko was incarcerated by the KGB. Terelya was haunted by KGB agents. In the Soviet Union, every citizen has to work. Those who cannot find employment can be jailed for parasitism. The Soviet authorities saw to it that he could not find work in his home town. As a religious activist, his writings had constantly been rejected by

Soviet publishers, and his works of art were criticized and deprecated by art critics. Therefore, he left his physician wife, Helen, and his family, and went to L'viv, where he was able to find a promise of employment. The KGB followed him, and on the following day the job was no longer available. He was arrested on December 24, 1982, and formally charged with parasitism, punishable by a two-year prison term.

For many days, Terelya's wife was unable to locate him. Finally, after going from one Investigative Bureau to another, she located him in the investigatory prison in Uzhorod.

Terelya expressed some of his feelings in a letter to the president of the Central Committee of German Catholics in West Germany. He wrote:

"While a man has the strength to rebel and to protest, he is still alive. My personal destiny closely follows the destiny of my people, which is that of Golgotha. But every ordeal has its end, and we are also waiting for the end of our Way of the Cross, after which comes the Resurrection.

"I am 39 years old and I have spent 18 of these years in prison camps and psychiatric prison hospitals of the vast Communist Empire. My great crime is that I am a Christian! Every Christian should know that Communism is not a result of the natural development of man, but a distortion of man's way of life, a complete destruction of Christian humanism. Therefore, we have the right to rebel, the right given to us by our own nature. We, as Christians, cannot sacrifice the truth for a transient peace with Communism.

"The Byzantine Catholic Church was, and still is, an Underground Church. Is it not difficult to believe that after twenty centuries a certain part of the human race is still forced to worship Christ secretly? I still do not know why they arrested me, but the fact is that they did arrest me and that they may even kill me. Two months ago, Lieut. Colonel Mykhajlo M. Dziamko, an officer of the District Headquarters of the KGB in Transcarpathia, said to me: 'We are handling this case with kid gloves. No one is going to find out in the West what is going on. They start to become worried in the West and make some fuss about it.' This is a true face of 'humane Communism.'

"In order to intimidate me, they killed my younger brother, Boris, on June 10, 1982. The murder was sanctioned by the Transcarpathian District authorities of the KGB. Immediately after the murder of my brother, a campaign of terror against my family began—searches, slander, threats... KGB agents told my mother that it was her elder son's turn next. What called for this hatred and cruelty towards me on the part of the KGB? My 'guilt' lay in the fact that my wife and I openly went to the Roman Rite Catholic Church, since our own, the Byzantine Catholic Church, had been liquidated and thus we publicly showed our opposition to the authorities."

The District Procurator in Irshava authorized the KGB to search Terelya's home and to confiscate all religious literature and human-rights material. Agents arrived late in the evening, broke down the door to the apartment, and searched it all night. They neglected to sign their names on a written report of the search. Allegedly a large quantity of human-rights material, books, letters, etc. were confiscated.

On April 12, 1983, Terelya was tried and sentenced to one year in prison. A Russian Orthodox human rights activist, Yelena Sannikova, had written a moving defense of Terelya and an appeal for aid to Pope John Paul II. This letter was widely publicized, and caused the attention of the Free World to be directed to the Terelya case. Therefore, his sentence was light. After his release, however, his defender was jailed for a year.

After his release from prison, Terelya started the publication of a religious underground paper, *The Chronicle*, in which he began to expose the continuing persecution of the Greek Catholics by the Soviet authorities. In the August 1984 issue, he wrote "The Russians in all probability will arrest me again. I expect soon to be arrested... I am ready for the worst..."

In order to escape the Soviet security, Terelya moved to the outskirts of L'viv, where he hoped to stay out of sight. The KGB soon discovered his new address, however, and unexpectedly broke into his apartment, confiscating all the material he had collected for forthcoming issues of *The Chronicle,* and his two typewriters. Fortunately he was not at home at the time of the surprise raid, and to escape arrest he went into hiding.

Terelya's health had been previously seriously impaired, and due to the intense winter cold he became sick and had to enter the sanatorium near L'viv. There, on February 8, 1985, he was located and arrested by the KGB. In spite of a high fever, he was taken to prison. Since he was not willing to "confess" or to inform on his supporters, he was given several months of "treatment" at the psychiatric prison.

Terelya wrote to his wife from prison in February of 1985, "Dear Olenka! If possible, please, do not cry. Remember the words of Jesus, who said: 'You will be hated because of my name. But those who will persevere till the end will be saved' (Mk. 13:13). Yes, because of His name! He also said, 'When men will take you to court, do not worry about what to say! (Mk. 13:11). Our children will grow up and live free from the Communist prejudices, free from hatred of Christ, and of their own people. A man, if he so desires, can remain free even behind the prison bars. They [the Soviets] have lost, though the KGB is repressing the Greek Catholic movement everywhere with great hatred and malice.... God be with you."

Finally, on August 20, 1985, Terelya was tried by the Soviet Regional Court in Uzhorod and sentenced to seven years in labor camp of strict regime and five years of exile for his underground religious activities.

On October 31, 1985, a joint Congressional Letter was sent to Soviet leader Mikhail Gorbachev, protesting the imprisonment of Terelya and calling for his release on humanitarian grounds.

Terelya was released in February of 1987. In September, he

and his family were allowed to leave the Soviet Union for Canada, where he went to receive medical treatment. He suffers from heart, liver and blood-pressure problems. He stated, "My liver became huge because of the 'cocktails' of drugs they injected daily as punishment in the psychiatric prison when I would not collaborate."

In an interview in Rome in the fall of 1987, Joseph Terelya expressed his hopes that the Soviet authorities are preparing to recognize the five-million-strong Byzantine Rite Ukrainian Catholic church. In August of 1987, he had delivered an appeal to Gorbachev, which was signed by 2 bishops, 23 priests, 12 monks, and 174 lay Catholics. The appeal also was sent to the Vatican.

When asked what is the root of his faith, which has been tested in so many prisons, Joseph Terelya replied, "I believe in the Gospels, and I want to live them."

Joseph Terelya. Photo courtesy of Rev. A. Pekar.

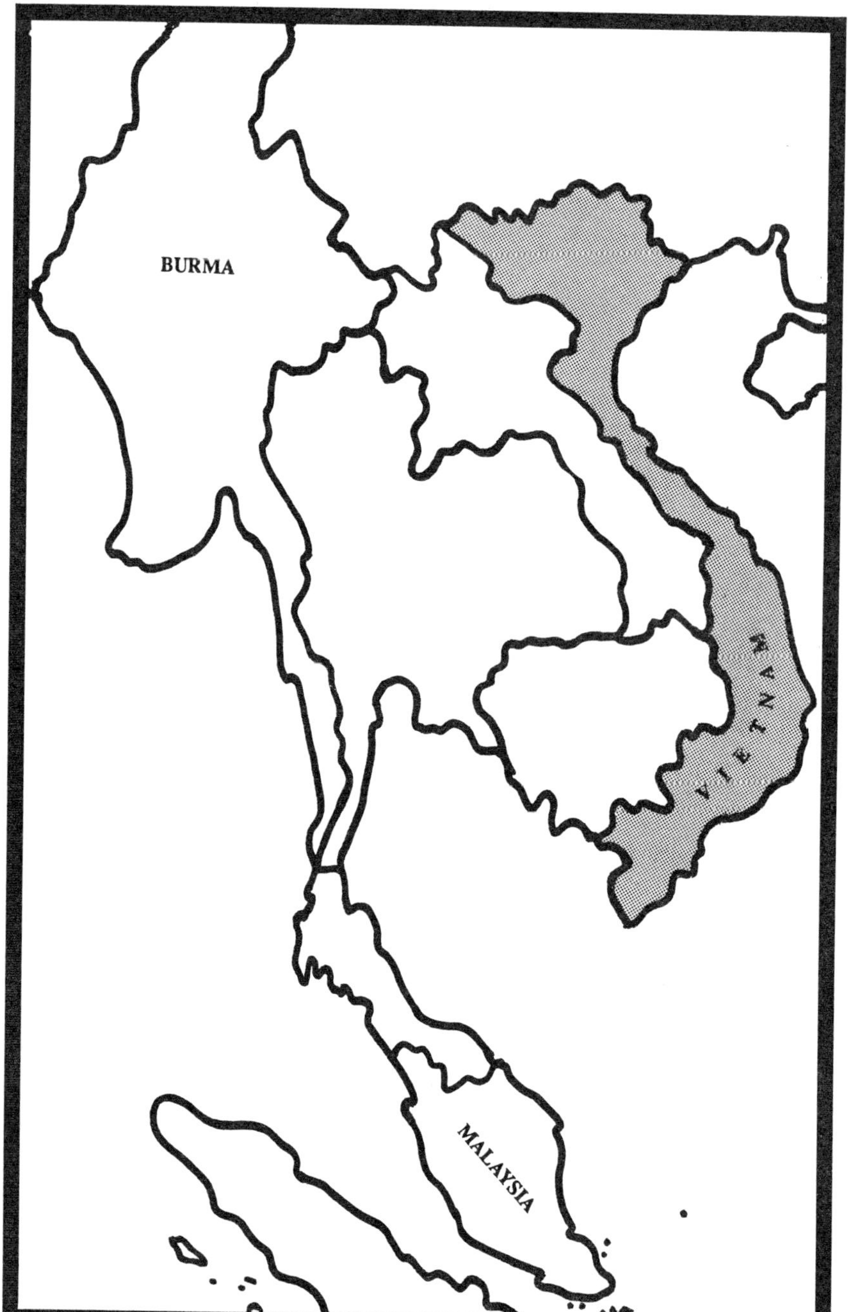

BURMA
VIETNAM
MALAYSIA

Vietnam

Although the government of Vietnam tolerates the existence of religious groups and tolerates some religious services, it has consistently attempted to divide and control the prominent religions. It sees religious groups as potential political opposition. The publishing of religious material and the training of new clergy is blocked. Membership in the communist party is required for political, educational, and economic advancement in Vietnam; thus Christians and other religious adherents are effectively discriminated against. Refugees from the country have reported regarding the continual government harassment, especially of the Catholic church. Reportedly, there are over one hundred Catholic priests confined in re-education camps. Others are confined in remote villages under house arrest. Many former military chaplains of all faiths have been confined since the mid-seventies. Consistent and credible reports of the severity of conditions in the re-education camps have filtered to the West. Conditions are brutal, and a significant number of deaths occur due to malnutrition, exhaustion and other unnatural causes.

    Police surveillance is constant on Catholic priests and nuns. The authorities require most religious to work full time in secular occupations, thereby limiting the time available for their religious work. The authorities have restricted communication between the rural parishes and their bishops. Additionally, they have restricted ordinations of new clergy. Although six seminaries were, in theory, reopened in 1980, none of the candidates met the criteria for enrollment. One former seminarian reported that no Catholic priest has been ordained since then.

Catholics must apply for and receive permission to attend religious services. The government routinely denies half of these applications, and in addition schedules required "voluntary" work during the time of regular church services. In some parts of the country, regulations dictate that daily Masses must be scheduled before six a.m. or after six p.m., and that all sermons must be cleared by the local police. Bibles may not be printed or imported, and members of different parishes may not hold joint meetings. No repairs may be made to church structures without permission from the government, and some churches have become completely unusable as applications for repairs are consistently denied.

Catholics are required to register with the authorities, and are discriminated against in employment. This has caused a gradual but steady decrease in the size of the Catholic congregations since the mid-seventies.

In the southern part of the country, the Catholic church seems to have survived most successfully in the cities, although the church's teaching role has been severely restricted. Many churches and all but one seminary in the south have been closed. In the central part of the country, thousands of Catholics have been relocated and forced to work on government projects. In 1982 the Catholic Patriotic Association was created in an attempt to weaken the church ties to the papacy, but the great majority of clergy and church members have ignored this attempt to develop a national Catholic church. In February of 1987, the Catholic Archbishop of Hue, Philippe Nguyen Kim Dien, was questioned by the police. His assistant was believed to be still in detention. The archbishop has been in conflict with the authorities due to his hostility to the Committee of Patriotic Catholics, and for his defense of two nuns who were arrested in 1985 while in possession of letters he had written.

The Protestant churches have also been harassed and restricted. In the highlands, all of the Protestant churches and their only seminary have been closed. In other parts of the country, church buildings have been appropriated by the government for various public buildings. The evangelicals who have been permitted to hold services are constantly harassed, and at least one group has been reportedly forbidden to meet.

Due to severe religious persecution as well as other factors, many Vietnamese have emigrated from the country both legally and clandestinely. Thousands of lives have been lost in this exodus. It is almost impossible to get detailed information or statistics from the country, but in 1982 Aid to the Church in Need listed 132 priests still held in camps, and 14 were known to have died. By 1986, about 300 of the country's 2,000 priests and religious were in detention or under house arrest. A communist party directive calls for the "merciless annihilation" of "reactionary" priests.

Religious orders have been disbanded, and a party document described the Jesuits as "the biggest, richest, most intelligent and strongest gang, containing the most dangerous CIA elements." The order has been singled out for special attacks. In 1983, thirteen of their priests and voluntary lay helpers were given prison sentences. After four arrests in 1985, there are only two Jesuit houses left in Vietnam.

Bishops consecrated since 1975 are not recognized by the state, and have been sent to re-education camps. The outspoken Bishop of Hue, Philippe Nguyen Kim Dien, has been forbidden to visit his parishes since 1984. Only three of the country's thirty-five bishops were allowed to make the 1985 ad limina visit to Rome.

Between May and July of 1987, a number of religious were arrested near Ho Chi Minh City. Father Dominic Tran Dinh Thu was arrested and jailed as a subversive. About forty of his order's priests and brothers were put under house arrest.

GERMAN DEMOCRATIC REPUBLIC
POLAND
CZECHOSLOVAKIA
HUNGARY
ROMANIA
YUGOSLAVIA
BULGARIA

Yugoslavia

The government of Yugoslavia officially encourages atheism, but the country remains multireligious, with a majority of the believers being Roman Catholic. Although freedom to practice religion is a constitutional guarantee, proselytizing is prohibited. This prohibition is often ignored, however, with few reprisals.

The different religious groups have vigorous publishing apostolates and Bibles are readily available. Although new church construction requires consent of government authorities, nearly all religious groups are building new facilities.

In 1986, a number of large religious gatherings happened without incident, and large-scale pilgrimages by both domestic and foreign Catholics are allowed at Medugorje.

Although services are allowed for the different religions, believers face possible discrimination. Party members may not publicly take part in the sacraments. Constraints on the religious education of children vary from region to region. Conflicts between the government and religious communities often develop if the religious groups become too political or nationalist in their activities. The Catholic church has been criticized by the government for its alleged support of Croatian nationalism and political activism.

The Serbian Orthodox church has been criticized for its alleged Serbian nationalism. In 1986, the Serbian Orthodox priest Sava Nedeljkovic was sentenced to a short prison term for supposedly having heard confession and given the last rites in a private home without receiving advance permission. In that case, Serbian Orthodox spokesmen, the Catholic press and the Belgrade news magazine *NIN* publicly accused the authorities of having gone too far.

Threats to the Church in the United States

by Stephen Dunham

Four police cars pulled into the church parking lot. The officers strode into the church, interrupted the Sunday-morning service then in progress, and served summonses to fifteen members of the congregation. [1]

* * *

In another incident, a seventy-two-year-old bishop was dragged across the pavement to a waiting police bus. Journalists trying to photograph the scene had their cameras confiscated and the film exposed. [2, 3]

Another man arrested said later, "They handcuffed my arms behind my back and dragged me away. I remember praying three Our Fathers out loud. One cop shouted in my ear, 'Stop that Our Father.'" [4]

A woman watching nearby and praying her rosary was thrown to the ground (she was sixty-four years old). She later testified, "[A policeman] grabbed my arms and shoved his riot stick across my back, twisting my wrists so that I screamed in pain. Then he put metal handcuffs on me." [5] At the police station, she said, two officers dragged her by her knees.

Also arrested that day was a seventy-four-year-old priest.

"They were sadistic," he said. "I have never seen such deliberate brutality. . . . They beat him [another priest]. When they brought him back his eyes were puffed and swollen, almost closed. His cheeks and face were swollen, his forehead cut. He definitely had been beaten up. His wrists bore cuts from the tight handcuffs." [6]

* * *

These events took place not behind the Iron Curtain, but in the United States of America in 1989. The interrupted church service was at the New Creation Community in Virginia Beach, Virginia. The violent arrests were in West Hartford, Connecticut.

Both events were part of a harsh governmental response to Operation Rescue, one of the most militant (but totally nonviolent) groups in the Christian church in America. While Operation Rescue's trespassing tactics are usually considered illegal by the courts (although in at least one instance a judge has ruled that trespassing to save a human life is not illegal; at least one other judge resigned rather than judge rescuers technically guilty), it is significant that Operation Rescue has provoked wholesale trampling of First Amendment rights.

The woman praying her rosary was not participating in the rescue, nor were the journalists arrested at West Hartford. And many of those arrested have been given especially rough treatment on account of their openly professed Christianity. William F. Buckley commented on the arrests at West Hartford: "Many of the victims screamed involuntarily, others sobbed. The police laughed and mocked them: 'Jesus isn't helping you,' one policeman told a praying rescuer, 'Call out for Satan.' " [7]

Writing about the assault on civil liberties in West Hartford, Catholic journalist Richard Cowden-Guido cited "eyewitness accounts of physical punishment against prisoners who pray together, which prison guards have forbidden them to do.

"The only protestors in America subject to this contemptible deprivation of rights are those who choose to protest abortion." [8]

Armando Valladares, U.S. Ambassador to the United Nations Commission on Human Rights, condemned the police brutality against rescuers, citing affidavits and photographic and videotaped evidence he had personally examined. "These abuses against nonviolent citizens," he said in a March 1990 statement, "constitute a clear and dangerous pattern of religious and political persecution." [9]

The wave of police violence began with a week of rescues at Atlanta abortion facilities during the 1988 Democratic National Convention in that city. The brutality spread to Denver, where three rescuers required hospital treatment after arrest, and Sacramento, where police used Mace—according to Sacramento attorney Cyrus Zal, "in total violation of California law. They even used it against a mother and her baby." [10]

In Los Angeles, "The commanding officer on the scene ordered his men to employ indiscriminate pain compliance on all rescuers regardless of sex or age," according to Operation Rescue founder Randall Terry. "Our women and elderly had their arms twisted, their fingers bent, their backs stepped upon.... One woman's arm was broken. Another man blacked out from the pain and was removed from the scene in an ambulance. Many had two fingers shoved up their nostrils as policeman lifted them by their noses. Others had knuckles pressed into their eye sockets." [11] The charge: misdemeanor trespass.

Perhaps the most shocking treatment of rescuers documented [12] thus far occurred following a rescue in Pittsburgh. No food was served to those arrested until up to thirty-three hours after their arrest. The Salvation Army arrived prepared to feed the rescuers but was turned away. The men were sent to the Mayview mental institution and the women were taken to the Allegheny County Jail, where the abuse reached an unholy crescendo.

One woman testified that the guards took away "anything that was prolife or religious.... rosaries, they took them, ripped them apart and threw them in the trash.... I even saw one of the guards take a Bible and throw it in the trash." [13]

Another woman was dragged up five flights of concrete stairs. She testified, "I had had an asthma attack in the holding cell." After being dragged upstairs, "I was taken around to a landing, and my bra was pulled up, and my shirt was totally pulled up, and my coat that had been taken off when I'd been searched earlier was put over my head, and one of the guards, and I don't know which one he was, punched me in the chest . . . [others] also punched me in both breasts, and [one] also started feeling with his hands and laughing . . . I heard the guards making threats of rape and all kinds of sexual acts against the women and at one point, one of the guards even put his hands down one of the girls' pants . . . the warden was watching all of this." [14]

Some of the women were subjected to more than one strip search, sometimes in front of male guards.

In the summer of 1989 the U.S. Civil Rights Commission at first refused to investigate the violence against Operation Rescue participants (on the grounds that Operation Rescue was protesting abortion, which is beyond the commission's domain) but later agreed to place it on their agenda. Civil Rights Commission chairman William Allen wrote to U.S. Attorney General Richard Thornburgh, ". . . the commission is precluded from addressing the abortion issue, but discrimination in the administration of justice is well within our jurisdiction." [15]

Assistant Attorney General James Turner's response included the comment that some allegations were being investigated by the FBI, and that the Attorney General's office was requesting that the FBI investigate "allegations that police and correctional officers purposely tried to conceal their identities by removing their badges and allegations that women were strip searched in front of male guards." [16]

Why has a Christian nonviolent protest movement brought such a savage backlash? Can it be isolated from the experiences of the rest of the church, or is it symptomatic of a sea change in the relationship of church and state?

First let us look at the causes of persecution. "Why did the Scribes and Pharisees have this man [Christ] put to death?" asked Rev. Robert D. Smith in *The Other Side of Christ.* [17] Why was Christ "hated so much that His enemies went to great lengths to have Him put to death? Christ himself told us. ... 'The world ... does hate me/ because of the evidence I bring against it/ that what it does is evil.'"

"Why is the Church hated and persecuted?" asked Rev. Smith. " ... in short, because of the evidence they [the Church] bring against the world that what it does is evil." [18]

When the church is faithful to its mission, clashes are inevitable. "There is a divine law which takes priority over civil law," wrote John Cardinal O'Connor, archbishop of New York. "It's the law which forbids the direct taking of innocent human life...." [19] The cardinal was writing about one of his auxiliary bishops, Austin Vaughan, defending Bishop Vaughan's participation in Operation Rescue. "If he has to miss a Sunday Mass or a Confirmation because he's in jail, I'll be proud to fill in," wrote Cardinal O'Connor.

Bishop Vaughan was both the first bishop to be arrested in a rescue and the first to be jailed, "indeed probably the first to go to jail for any reason in a long time" [20] (in the U.S.), according to the prolife magazine *ALL About Issues.* Other Catholic bishops have since joined the rescue movement, including Bishop Albert Ottenweiler of Steubenville, Ohio, and Bishop Paul Dudley of Sioux Falls, South Dakota, and the Catholic clergy have not been alone in battling abortion with civil disobedience. More pastors were arrested in 1988 in Atlanta than in the Soviet Union, according to American Life League.

While the issue of shedding innocent blood (through abortion, infanticide and euthanasia) has brought some Christians into conflict with the law, this is not the only issue on which the church finds itself at odds with the government.

Virgil Blum, president of the Catholic League for Religious

and Civil Rights, has concluded that the Supreme Court is hostile to religion. In an August 1989 essay in the league's newsletter, he cited two cases involving remedial education taught by public school teachers in private school classrooms.

In Pennsylvania, wrote Blum, "The law provided that teachers of the remedial classes were to be public school teachers, under the exclusive control and direction of the state, and that classrooms were to be totally sanitized of all religious symbols, statements and pictures.... But the Supreme Court was not happy! Scrutinizing the public school teachers—Protestants, Catholics, Jews and nonbelievers—the Court said . . . they 'have the potential' to indoctrinate the children in religion. To protect the children against possible religious indoctrination, the Court said, the states had to provide 'continuing surveillance' to police the public school teachers.

"But, ruled the Court, such policing of state teachers in Catholic schools constitutes an excessive entanglement between church and state....

"This denial of remedial education, said the Chief Justice [Burger, in his dissenting opinion], is a violation of the 'free exercise of religious belief' and 'a denial of equal protection.' " [21]

" 'It borders on paranoia . . .' " said Burger.

In its zeal to apply the First Amendment prohibition against government "establishment of religion," the Supreme Court has attempted to erect a "wall of separation between Church and State"—an idea ascribed to Thomas Jefferson, but not in the Constitution. This has led not only to an absence of government support of religion, but frequently to an end of government cooperation with religion. Government relief activities such as adoption services and aid to the poor that once were performed in cooperation with the churches are now being totally secularized, while new programs, such as ones designed to promote chastity among teens, are being implemented without church participation.

Removal of government funding for church charitable

activities, however, does not constitute open interference with the churches. More pernicious are the government attempts to impose secular standards on the activity of religious institutions, as in the court order that required Georgetown University, a Catholic institution in Washington, D.C., to grant official standing to student homosexual groups. The American government of the late twentieth century, especially the judiciary, seeks to establish public policy without regard to religiously based values.

In Roe v. Wade, the 1973 Supreme Court decision legalizing abortion on demand through all nine months of pregnancy, "for the first time in American jurisprudence, it was explicitly stated that it is possible to address these issues of ultimate importance without any reference to the Judeo-Christian tradition that has always been the primary source of public values in America," wrote Lutheran pastor Richard John Neuhaus, director of the Institute on Religion and Public Life. [22]

The effort to eliminate Christian values from the formulation of public policy is also reflected, and sometimes led by, much of the mass media. Rev. Donald Wildmon, a Methodist minister and head of the American Family Association, has published volumes of documentation showing that by and large the mass media, especially network T.V., ridicule Christianity. Although this kind of private persecution is not government-authorized, Gailfred Boller Sweetland of the Catholic League for Religious and Civil Rights contends that "freedom of speech is a sham freedom if freedom of the press or of speech makes ridicule, defamation, belittling of religion acceptable." [23]

The current situation seems to point up the necessity for action," she continued, "decisive and intelligent action, on the part of religious believers. Otherwise the ridicule and defamation of religion, which has had, and continues to have, a chilling effect on the free exercise rights of religious believers, will only continue, and will doubtless increase." [24]

* * *

Father Norman Weslin, while being held at "The Farm," an Atlanta prison, had an opportunity to say Mass for about 125 other prisoners in the prison yard. Guards interrupted him and ordered him inside. He resumed saying Mass in a dormitory but was hustled away by a prison guard. Rev. Weslin was reprimanded by the warden and placed in solitary confinement.

* * *

"I was arrested and held in jail overnight for singing Christian songs on public property outside the city jail with 20 others!" wrote Randall Terry. "They locked me up, without telling me what I was charged with. Eventually they told me, 'Disorderly Conduct.' Can you imagine? I was arrested and jailed for singing Christian hymns on public property! Are we in Leningrad, or Binghamton? Russia, or the USA? Where is our nation heading?" [25]

1 *Rescue Newsbrief,* June/July 1989, pp. 1, 3.

2 Interview with eyewitness, Oct. 28, 1989.

3 Mark Jahne, "Operation Rescue Results in 261 Arrests; Police Brutality Charged," *West Hartford News,* June 22, 1989, pp. 1, 18.

4 Henry V. King, "Mayor, Town Council Defend West Hartford Police," *The Wanderer,* July 27, 1989, p. 1.

5 Ibid., p. 7.

6 Ibid., p. 1.

7 *New York Daily News,* July 1989.

8 Richard Cowden-Guido, National Operation Rescue Movement news release, June 23, 1989.

9 "Rights Leader Decries Brutality," *Human Life International Reports,* May 1990, p. 11.

10 Arthur J. Brew, "Police Violence Against Rescues Investigated," *The Wanderer,* Aug. 3, 1989, p. 1.

11 Operation Rescue newsletter, Mar. 28, 1989, p. 3.

12 The Pittsburgh incidents were investigated and reported on by U.S. Civil Rights Commission Chairman William Allen and by New York Congressman Guy Molinari (reported in *30 Days,* October 1989), in addition to the journalistic reports cited below.

13 Suzanne M. Rini, "The Abortion Empire Strikes Back," *Fidelity,* June 1989, p. 26.

14 Ibid., p. 27.

15 Arthur J. Brew, "U.S. Civil Rights Commission Defers Action on Charges of Police Brutality Against Rescuers," *The Wanderer,* Aug. 10, 1989, p. 1.

16 Ibid., p. 2.

17 Rev. Robert D. Smith, *The Other Side of Christ* (Avon, NJ: Magnificat Press, 1987), pp. 1, 2.

18 Ibid., pp. 2, 3.

19 John Cardinal O'Connor, "More, Fisher ... and Vaughan," *Catholic New York,* Nov. 24, 1988.

20 "Bishop Vaughan Stands Firm, Does Time; Cardinal O'Connor Hints He May Join the Rescue Movement," *ALL About Issues,* Feb. 1989, p. 7.

21 Rev. Virgil C. Blum, "Is the Court Hostile to Religion?" 2Catholic League Newsletter, Aug. 1989, p. 8.

22 Pastor Richard John Neuhaus, "Moral Leadership in Post-Secular America," *Catholic League Newsletter,* Vol. 16, No. 8.

23 Gailfred Boller Sweetland, "Where Freedoms Clash," *Catholic League Newsletter,* Vol. 16, No. 4, p. 4.

24 Ibid.

25 *Rescue Newsbrief,* Aug. 1989, p. 2.

Selected Bibliography

Department of State. *Country Reports on Human Rights Practices for 1986.* United States Government Printing Office: Washington, 1987.

Department of State. *Country Reports on Human Rights Practices for 1985.* United States Government Printing Office: Washington, 1986.

Foy, Felician. *1988 Catholic Almanac.* Our Sunday Visitor Publishing Division: Huntington, Indiana, 1987.

Broun, Janice A. "Church Progressively Undermined in Vietnam." *Our Sunday Visitor* 21 Aug. 1986, p. 20.

"Modern Martyrs." *Our Sunday Visitor* 13 Sept. 1987.

"Scholar Claims Martyrdom of Christians Increased in 20th Century." *Christian News* 25 May 1987.

Novo Pena, Silvia. "Mass for Prisoners Unearths Memories of Cuban Captivity." *Texas Catholic Herald* 27 Mar. 1987.

"Slain Missioners in Love with God and People." *Texas Catholic Herald* 12 Dec. 1980.

Egenolf, Fred. "Pauline Fathers Honor Slain Priest." *Daily Intelligencer* 3 Nov. 1985.

Grant, Kevin. *The Valiant Shepherd* July, 1986.

Fox, John. "Do You Hear the Bells, Father Jerzy?" *Reader's Digest* Vol. 127, Dec. 1985, p. 65.

An America's Watch Report. *Guatemala: A Nation of Prisoners.* America's Watch Committee: New York, 1984.

Lernoux, Penny. *Cry of the People.* Doubleday: New York, 1980.

If the Grain of Wheat Dies... Fr. Francis Xavier Chu Shu-Teh, S.J. (undated booklet c. 1984; no author or place of publication is given).

Pekar, A., O.S.B.M. *You Shall Be Witnesses Unto Me.* Byzantine Seminary Press: Pittsburgh, 1985.

Pekar, A. O.S.B.M. *Our Martyred Bishop Romzha.* Byzantine Seminary Press: Pittsburgh, 1977.

Pekar, A. O.S.B.M. *Bishop Hopko, Confessor of Faith.* Byzantine Seminary Press: Pittsburgh, 1979.

Pekar, A. O.S.B.M. *Confessor of Our Times.* Byzantine Seminary Press: Pittsburgh, 1977.

Pekar, A. O.S.B.M. "Joseph Terelya, Prisoner of Christ" (pamphlet materials, unpublished).

San Pedro, Bishop Enrique. Diocese of Galveston-Houston. Interview with author, August 1987.

Chronicle of the Catholic Church in Lithuania Lithuanian Catholic Religious Aid. Brooklyn, NY. No. 70.

Organizations Supporting the Persecuted Church

Aid to the Church in Need

PO Box 576
Deer Park, NY 11729

PO Box 11
Eastwood, NSW 2122
Australia

PO Box 250
Montreal, PQ H3P 3C5
Canada

Holy Trinity Abbey, Kilnacrott
Ballyjamesduff, County Cavan
Ireland

124 Carshalton Rd.
Sutton, Surrey SM1 4RL
United Kingdom

Cardinal Mindszenty Foundation

PO Box 11321
St. Louis, MO 63105

Free the Fathers

>1120 Applewood Circle
>Signal Mountain, TN 37377

Human Life International

>7845-E Airpark Rd.
>Gaithersburg, MD 20879
>(301) 670-7884

>Branch offices in Argentina, Austria, Brazil, Canada, Chile, Ecuador, El Salvador, India, Italy, Kenya, Mexico, Paraguay, Peru, Philippines, Poland, Scotland, Singapore, South Africa, Sweden, Trinidad, Uruguay, West Germany, Yugoslavia

Lithuanian Information Center

>351 Highland Blvd.
>Brooklyn, NY 11207

Keston College

>PO Box 1310
>Framingham, MA 01701

Persecuted Church Commission

>PO Box 1340
>Kingston, NY 12401

Puebla Institute

>910 17th St. NW, Suite 409
>Washington, DC 20006